MAN The Greatest of Miracles

MAN The Greatest of Miracles

An Answer to the Sexual Counter-Evolution

by
Dr. med. Siegfried Ernst

translated by
Sister Margretta Nathe, O.S.B.
Mary Rosera Joyce

THE LITURGICAL PRESS
Collegeville, Minnesota

MAN — THE GREATEST OF MIRACLES is the authorized English version of *Das grösste Wunder ist der Mensch*, published by Martin Verlag/Walter Berger, Buxheim/Allgäu.

Printed by The North Central Publishing Company, St. Paul, Minnesota, U.S.A.

ISBN 0-8146-0905-8.

FOREWORD

Any pro-life traveller in Europe will soon recognize the name of Dr. Siegfried Ernst. No one in Germany, and perhaps in the whole of Europe, has defended the unborn and the medical profession with tongue and pen like this indefatigable Lutheran philosopher-theologian-doctor from Ulm. His qualifications are superb; his deep interests in the pro-life movement stem right out of a resistance to the anti-life policies of Hitler and his early involvement in the Moral Rearmament Movement.

This English translation of his German best seller will greatly enrich the understanding of what is really at stake in resisting the evils of contraception-abortion-euthanasia unleashed upon the modern world. The book also contains not a few invaluable insights on human sexuality and the so-called sexual revolution. Everyone, above all parents, involved in marriage and family life education will find herein answers to many puzzling questions in a sensuous culture.

Anyone who digests Dr. Ernst's observations will have learned greatly.

The author is one of the founders of World Doctors Who Respect Life and a member of the Lutheran Wuerttemberg Synod.

Dr. Paul Marx
The Human Life Center
St. John's University
Collegeville, Minnesota

INTRODUCTION

The greatest wonder of all is man! That is one of the most important disclosures of the present century!

Not only did man produce the atom bomb and explore the surface of the moon; he also made discoveries in the microcosm of elementary particles and of organic molecules. He began to illumine the recesses of the unconscious, sought to unveil the mysteries of evolution, to explain the chemical and electronic reactions of the brain and to recognize the nature of communication. Thus an increasingly confusing multiplicity of phenomena became available to us. And still we have not been able to answer the question about final causes and goals, about destiny and meaning of the whole, any more satisfactorily than did our forbears.

The question about the meaning of being human determines the character of a society in all its ramifications and purposes. In a world diminished in size by technology, the problem of common basis of order and of universally binding system of goals has become the first question of survival. Unless there is a correct response, mankind has no future.

Is man simply the product of unplanned, haphazard mutations and of the "pressure of selection," that is, the end-product of the struggle for existence? Is he just matter that no longer has anything mysterious about it, that recognizes no purpose and obeys blind laws — a being without values, and thus quite liable to be manipulated, ruled, liquidated at the behest and requirement of those who happen to be in power? Or is the goal of man's development that of being the partner — indeed, the "likeness" — of God, possessed of a sublime destiny and an eternal meaning and value?

This hitherto unbridgeable opposition in the self-image of mankind has become the source of a profound conflict. On the one hand, certain groups in society assume the right to be allowed to manipulate arbitrarily the begetting of man, indeed, to liquidate the already developing human life, which is construed as being only a materialistic "clump of cells" or as merely the product of remarkable "accidents"; on the other hand, counter groups defend the sacredness of all human life.

Some modern regimes have made the materialistic concept of man the basis of their social institutions. As Western democracies liberated themselves from the more exalted meaning of life and from every sort of higher responsibility, their laws began to change accordingly. Laws that implied, practically and juridically, that man is more than a purely accidental congeries of materials and that placed his conception, his pre-natal growth, his birth, his education and formation to adulthood under careful protection were abolished.

Hence, in treating of the question of birth control and abortion, we are not dealing primarily with sexual, biological, psychological, medical or juridical aspects, but more immediately with the future of mankind on this planet Earth that has grown so small.

It is typical that all regimes with a materialistic concept of man and of human society, immediately upon assuming power, place the liquidation of the unborn under the arbitrary will of those who are pregnant, and thus express which of the two viewpoints (the human or the materialistic) is to determine the future of the world for them.

It is just as typical that these governments, once they are driven to recognize the catastrophe resulting from their abortion freedom, generally are unable to reverse their course. The only reason that could move the women and physicians of these countries to give up the practice of abortion, namely that it is the killing of human beings, is also the reason that would seriously compromise the larger materialistic view upon which the whole regime is based. The sacrifice of spiritual and religious positions of Christian thought regarding the jurisprudence of society is decisive for beginning the domination of society by the materialistic viewpoint regarding the nature of man and his right to existence.

Whoever wishes to occupy himself with the questions of birth control, "the right to a full sexual life" and abortion must know that these are only superficial symptoms of a more fundamental concept of man which must be examined first, and thereafter the question about correct laws and ordinances can be answered.

An attempt to establish a comprehensive view of the world appears hopeless if an ordinary physician undertakes it. In the face of the immense specialization and the complication of modern research and knowledge, he cannot hope to master the whole of the matter if he wishes to be a "specialist." I have no desire to add another to the many existing specialties, because I am of the opinion that today the ability to form a conspectus of the horizontal and vertical aspects of determined scientific, philosophical and political questions is more important than new special knowledge. Few professions are more suited for this task than that of the practicing physician who in his daily routine must constantly attempt to understand medical specialties as a whole and who, besides, stands in the midst of today's events. As a family physician, an industrial physician, etc., he gains greater insight into all strata of the population and their actual lives, their fears, hopes and goals, than any other professional. Besides, by reason of his scientific position, he occupies a place between the modern natural sciences and the intellectual sciences and forms in his person a bridge between them.

Such a physician is obliged to understand the material existence of man, his physical, chemical and biological reactions and interactions, together with the intellectual, spiritual, social, political and religious facets of human existence. He is responsible for the whole of life, not only for its chemical and physical appearances. He must know that this wholeness of life cannot be divided, cannot be separated into specialized fields, without doing violence to the whole. Consequently, he stands in need of a new medical orientation. He needs to grow beyond the one-sided chemical and physical consideration of human reality, and try to see these parts in the light of the whole of human existence.

Furthermore, the European physician is the bearer of a most magnificent humane and scientific tradition. Today, as never before, this tradition runs the risk of being perverted by ideological attacks against the spiritual and moral bases of the European medical profession. New attempts are being made to degrade the physician to a materialistic death-functionary of the current ideology. This trend began with the widespread error that the Pill is the answer to the problem of abortion, an idea that was clearly refuted in the memorandum of the district physicians' association of Ulm, together with the physicians of Ehingen and Calw (a total of 400 physicians, among them 45 university professors and 90% of the practicing gynecologists of Baden-Wuerttemberg). Years ago we already pointed out that making the Pill a consumer's article and a source of pleasure would lead to a decided mass sexual "liberation" and that the anti-baby campaign, after an initial possible reduction, would not substantially alter the number of abortions, since such means would strengthen the negative attitude against the child.

At the same time and quite independently, 140 Swedish physicians warned their king about the consequences of open sexuality, as well as of sexual instruction on birth control and sexual techniques.

Simultaneously 800 participants of the International Society on Nutrition Research, in a protest to the Ministry of Health, pointed out the danger of premature sexual activity and the early use of the Pill on the part of young girls, as well as the consequences for marital intercourse. Among the signers were very many professors of medicine and physicians who belonged to the scientific council of the Society.

Therefore, at present, the medical profession faces the dilemma either of supplying the populace with a better response to the modern sexual revolution than the present symptomatic struggle against abortions by prescribing pills, or of helplessly witnessing the corruption of the entire medical field and the loss of a medical and humane tradition going back thousands of years.

Such a response, as has been said, must concern itself not only with the symptoms of the crisis. In the long run, it is mindless to try to cure one evil with another. If we wish to save this dying people, we need a more profound diagnosis and a more radical therapy. If, in a normal middle-sized city like Ulm, there are today only two births for three deaths and if, besides, there is propaganda for abortion at will, then we are dealing with the suicide of a people, a condition clearly predicted (in the memorandum of Ulm) as the final result of the sexual revolution. When one considers the pertinacity with which government officials and legislators hold fast to their murderous ideas about freedom in the face of this situation, while defending pornography as a right of sexual psychopaths, and while departments of education draw even school children into the trend, then it becomes difficult to attribute such behavior only to stupidity and cowardice rather than to a systematically conceived plan that has for its goal the annihilation of this nation.

Hence, it is not by accident that European physicians who recognize this danger to their patients, to the entire medical profession, and to freedom itself are now organizing to develop the necessary diagnosis.

Within the framework of this united action to save Europe, my book came into being. Instead of emphasizing medical, biological or psychological details, it focuses on the ideological background of the present condition of the world and presents the basic requirements of human community from the viewpoint of the physician.

The first part of the book discusses the modern question of evolution and the particular problem of human development and counter-evolution. The second part is concerned with the specific nature of human sexuality and the norms of conduct for the future. And the third part discusses the movements and controversies in the Christian churches regarding the right order of human sexuality. This latter part is, at the same time, the confession of an Evangelical physician who, as a member of the Evangelical Synod of Wuerttemberg, as a long-time councillor of the city of Ulm, as part-time industrial physician, as participant in numerous international conferences, and not least, as the father of six children, attempts to point out a passable way through the jungle of confusion.

I do not claim at all to comprehend the contemporary situation in all its details, and I am always ready to be persuaded by better arguments. It is my conviction that no individual can express the whole of truth and of reality. I can only sketch the general direction and paint the picture in broad outlines. If a complete picture of a viable future is to result, innumerable stones still have to be set in the mosaic.

Siegfried Ernst, M.D.

Ulm, January 1974

SEGRETERIA DI STATO

Nr. 193.230

DAL VATICANO, 21. September 1971

Sehr geehrter Herr Dr. Ernst!

Bei Gelegenheit der Sonderaudienz vom 25.
August d. J. überreichten Sie Seiner Heiligkeit ne-
ben einigen Informationsschriften über Ihren mutigen
Kampf gegen den in der Öffentlichkeit immer bedroh-
licher um sich greifenden allgemeinen Sittenverfall
auch Ihre persönliche Studie über die Enzyklika "Humanae Vitae".

Der Heilige Vater hat mit besonderem Interes-
se in Ihre Ausführungen Einblick genommen und läßt
Ihnen für Ihr verständnisvolles und entschiedenes
Eintreten für die Lehraussagen dieses bedeutsamen
päpstlichen Dokumentes ein aufrichtiges Wort des
Dankes und der Anerkennung übermitteln. Er gibt dem
Wunsche Ausdruck, daß Ihre lobenswerten Bemühungen
mit dazu beitragen mögen, daß die sittlichen Grund-
sätze, die die Enzyklika "Humanae Vitae" erneut in
Erinnerung ruft und bekräftigt, bei allen Menschen
guten Willens eine immer bereitere Aufnahme finden.

Seine Heiligkeit erfleht Ihnen, sehr geehrter
Herr Doktor, für weiteres erfolgreiches Wirken sowie
auch Ihrer Familie von Herzen Gottes besonderen
Schutz und Segen.

Indem ich mich beehre, Sie hiervon zu unter-
richten, bin ich mit dem Ausdruck vorzüglicher Wert-
schätzung

Ihr sehr ergebener

J. Card. Villot

TABLE OF CONTENTS

Part One

The Miracle of Human Evolution 3
The Will to a Higher Meaning 4
The Meaning of Laws of Nature 5
The "Will Toward Meaning" 8
"Will to Pleasure" 13
Logotherapy 14
Evolution Toward Freedom 16
The Sexual Revolution 17
Sex Education and Counter-Evolution 19
Sex Acceleration in the Child 20
Counter-Evolution in the Husband 22
Counter-Evolution in the Wife 23
Sexual-Socialistic Counter-Evolution 25
Counter-Evolution in Art 27
Counter-Evolution in Ideology 29

Part Two

Human Sexuality and Its Norms 35
Premarital Sex 36
The Old Sex Morality No Longer Adequate . . . 41
The Prevention of Ovulation 44
The Decadent Re-evaluation of Masturbation . . . 45
The Effect of the "Pill" upon Premarital Chastity . . 47
Tolerance Toward Malignancy 48
Modern Sexuality as an Artificial Product . . . 49
"Degeneration Caused by Affluence" 49
Is Homosexuality Innate or Programmed after Birth? . . 52
The Aggressive Drive and the Sex Drive . . . 52
Temporary Receding of the Sex Drive . . . 54
Positive Aggression and Sexual Discipline . . . 54

xvi   *Contents*

Biological Indicators of Human Sexual Nature . . . 56
A Sense of Shame versus Pornography 57
Why Must Pornography Be Forbidden? 59
Imported "Sexual Freedom" 61
The Statement of the Medical Doctors of Ulm Is Verified . 63
Overcoming a Relative Old Morality 65
Points of Orientation for Spiritual-Moral Standards . . 67
The History of Man 67
The Political Point of Orientation 69
The Biological Point of Orientation 70
A Relevant Analogy 72
The Psychological Point of Orientation 73
Ideology-Neurosis 75
A False Cure for Neurosis 75
The Cross as the Answer to Neurosis 77
The Sociological Point of Orientation 79
Universally Binding Standards 81
Absolute Moral Standards 83
Modernizing the Penal Law 86

Part Three

The Encyclical *Humanae Vitae* 89
The Concept of "Nature" in *Humanae Vitae* . . . 91
Driven by Instinct? Directed by Knowledge? . . . 93
Unity and Synchronization in Human Sexuality . . 94
Natural and Unnatural Family Planning 95
Psychological-Moral Distinctions 96
The Bible and Contraception 98
Love Responds to Life 99
Attitudes Make a Difference 100
Wanted Children 101
The Counter-Evolution of Abortion 102
Crossing the Rubicon to Complete Sexual "Freedom" . 103
Human Sexual Nature 103
Perversion of the Value Scale 104
The "Nature" of Human Sexuality 106

The Super-Nature of Human Sexuality 108
The Church and the Counsel of the Laity 109
The Limits of Science 110
The Degeneration of Confession 111
The Real Meaning of Confession 112
Isolated Sex and Man's Relation with God . . . 113
Religious Infantilism 116
Transformation of Creative Energy 116
Contraception and the Sacramental Character of Marriage 117
Pope Paul VI and the Opposition 118
Faith and Science Are Complementary 119
The "Lesser Evil" Is Still an Evil 120
Abandonment of the Person to the "Pill" 121
Rajmohan Gandhi's View; The Pope Is Not Alone . . 122
Summary — A Path to Atheism in the Church . . . 124
Infallible Statements or Infallible Guides? . . . 125
The Limitations of Logic 126
The True Meaning of Infallibility 128
The Problem Is Not Infallibility 129
By Their Fruits You Will Know Them 132
"Infallible" Professors 134
Both Priest and Prophet 134
Personal Inspiration: An Alternative in a Conflict . . 136
Did the Pope Act Without Collegiality? 137
Humanae Vitae and the Question of Infallibility . . 138
A Decision for the Cross 139
Is *Humanae Vitae* for Protestants, Too? 141
The Encyclical and Inspiration 141
Host or "Pill"? 142
God or Chaos? 144
Appendix I 147
Appendix II 159
Appendix III 161
Appendix IV 168
Appendix V 170
Bibliographical References 197

MAN The Greatest of Miracles

Part One

The Miracle of Human Evolution

Today there is a worldwide explosion in scientific and technological knowledge; there is also a widespread breakdown in meanings, values, and moral structures. Mankind is shaken by great tensions and problems — it is even threatened with succumbing to annihilation. Never before was it possible, as it is now, to change, manipulate, suppress, misuse and radically deceive man, to take advantage of him or to liquidate him. Nor did man ever have so many possibilities for changing the earth into a paradise and for directing whole nations toward a common future. Must a catastrophe of unthinkable proportions come upon us only because we refuse to recognize our true destiny and, as individuals, families, nations and races, fail to take the necessary preventive action? In the face of present-day blindness and obstinacy, fanaticism and bewilderment, indifference, cowardice and corruption, all having a magnitude hardly seen in any generation before, it is difficult to realize that, of all beings which inhabit the solar system, this being "man" is the most wonderful and most inexplicable.

Man is a creature who, like countless others, originates from the fusion of two cells and their nuclei. He develops according to a definite plan that is established in chromosomes and genes. His design was part of a two-billion-year evolutionary process, including biological, cultural and spiritual development. He is the result of a unique, irreversible process which cannot be repeated in the same way.

Unlike all other known living creatures, man has the capacity for understanding himself and his world, for examining, analyzing and renewing himself. He not only can store knowledge in his memory but can retain it technically. Furthermore, he can accumulate and transmit this knowledge to future generations. He has the power either to plan and build the future, or consciously to destroy it. Only man can judge his own behavior, perceive his own motives and evaluate them. Even as a small child this human creature asks about the meaning of life and of things. In a special way he reveals the fundamental drive rooted in the finest structures of all existing beings: the "will to a higher meaning."

The Will to a Higher Meaning as the Basic Thrust of Life

The question "why" which a child spontaneously asks about things that exist expresses one of the essential behavior patterns which help to form human character. In man the primary tendency is to become conscious of what exists. This quality of life which is of a high order is possible only when drives of a lower order adapt themselves to the higher totality. Only insofar as the "building stones" of the lower order integrate themselves into the order of a living being with a higher quality, and respond to its superior purposes, do they enter into a new life and level of existence.

This principle of integrating lower drives into higher ones is the principle of evolution. It applies to all components, even the most elementary, which are part of a higher quality of existence. This is true of atoms, which unite to form molecules. These, in turn, unite to assume new, more complex qualities. But the larger units cannot be explained merely as the sum total of all their parts. The larger units can be explained only by the force of their own total quality.

An example of the principle of integration working toward higher life is the highly complex protein molecule. The structure of its "building stones," the amino acids, is dictated by DNA, and this structure appears in all human nuclei. DNA, bearing genetic information, determines the form, shape, function and behavioral patterns of the individual organism and the species. The existence of cells would be impossible without their ability to permit themselves to be integrated into a higher stage of organization, to tend to a "better quality of life" and to reproduce themselves. Even our own existence as human beings would not be possible without this same principle of integration. Because of this principle, there is a transition in quality from the nucleic acid protein molecules to living cells which again become part of an organ, then part of a system of organs in a body. In this latter system, the protein molecules receive entirely new qualities and functions as parts of a higher order.

Whatever is true of individual parts of an organism is true also of its drives. In his book *Das sogenannte Boese*, Konrad Lorenz tries to identify the basic animal drives and to reduce them to four separate major urges: the hunger drive, the sex drive, the aggressive drive and the escape drive.[1] He shows that all four drives serve the preservation and development of the individual animal, as well as of the species.

Like our body and its organs, these four drives must receive their human quality from our consciousness, sense of responsibility, will and spirit. Our person must be ordered, in turn, to a higher plan and quality of existence. Otherwise our drives will fail to be coordinated and meaningfully channelled; they will tend toward senseless destruction. It is obvious that all parts of our existence are capable of responding to impulses which originate in the superior whole. The form and the function of each cell of our bodies are determined by the impulses and orders which are constantly sent out from the control center. Indeed, even the molecules and elementary particles of our brain cells respond to our wills and execute orders which help us direct our bodies and control our thoughts.

Therefore, it goes against what we know to assume that man is an exception to the basic thrust of life that tends toward integration into a higher totality and quality of existence. To think that human life is such an exception is senseless, because we know we are able to respond to orders and impulses in a better way than lower beings. We know that our whole societal system of order and communal achievements is built upon this potential.

Furthermore, it is a special human quality to question the why and whither of our own existence . . . to seek a higher meaning and final goal. At the same time, we are the only being which does not have to follow the drive to a higher meaning. We can become critical and decide; we are able to make absurd choices. We need not behave instinctively like animals and plants in regard to evolution. We can choose counter-evolution. (*See Appendix I*).

The Meaning of Laws of Nature

Parts working together in a higher quality of existence do so according to definite patterns called laws of nature. Without them,

1 References are to the bibliography given on page 170ff.

life's higher forms and organisms are impossible. Man, the greatest organism, never would have been formed.

Laws in the realm of elementary parts, energy quanta and atoms are *physical laws*. Those laws which determine the working together of atoms within the higher forms of molecules are *chemical laws*. The patterns which determine the work of cells and organs in an organism are called *biological laws*. And finally, the laws which determine the higher quality of existence in family, community, business, commerce and politics are called *moral laws*.

The same principles which apply to physical and chemical laws apply to moral laws. For example, modern natural science discovered that the elements of nature hold to absolute patterns only according to statistical probability. This same quality of probability based on law can be detected in moral laws such as traffic regulations. An observer of the movement of traffic in a modern city, from a height of a few thousand meters, will recognize at once a definite speed limit and other rules. However, the closer he approaches, the better he can observe the individual vehicles. Then he will notice that some move contrary to traffic laws; for example, some do not observe the speed limit. By comparing this observation with other similar instances, he will also notice that the stricter the laws are, the fewer violations of traffic there will be.

According to the modern discovery of statistical probability, miracles are not regarded as breakdowns in the laws of nature, but as exceptions to these laws. Miracles are recognized as evidence of spiritual patterns or ways of directing the elements of nature. They are no longer regarded as unthinkable, but rather as theoretically conceivable beyond the scope of natural science.

If miracles are not breakdowns in the laws of nature, neither are moral laws which originate from the spirit. Moral norms can be considered as laws of nature on the level of human society. Konrad Lorenz defines this issue in his book *Das sogenannte Boese*, on page 342, where he tries to answer Kant's "categorical question," namely, "Can I raise the maxims of my actions to a law of nature or is this contrary to reason?" He tries to prove, through norms of moral behavior, the identity of certain purely instinctive patterns of behavior inasmuch as they fulfill the preservation of the species. "Whatever is contrary to reason shows up only in the abnormal functioning of an instinct. It is the task of the categorical question to discover this relation between moral norms and laws of nature, and it is the task of the consequent imperative to affirm this relation. Instincts which function correctly, that is, according to their meaningful task of preserving the species and of furthering life, cannot contradict what is reasonable. If one asks, 'Can I raise the maxims of my conduct to the level of the laws of nature?' the answer is definitely *yes*, because that is the way it is!"

The right functioning of human instincts (on the pre-moral level), as well as their wrong functioning, depends on the right or wrong moral guidance given the instinct by the human being or group concerned. This moral guidance is determined by the ideal of our final end toward which we order our lives. If this self-ordering is done correctly, there will be no conflict between moral laws and laws of nature.

Our cooperation with our call to a higher quality of being is made possible by laws and rules. But a price is always paid. A higher quality of existence is attained only by sacrificing our former level of "freedom" and assuming a firm responsibility. This law of sacrificing the lower for the higher is valid on all levels of existence. But the voluntary, conscious action of a human being ordering himself according to laws of nature, rules of life and absolute norms represents a special limiting of freedom and sacrificing of independence. Actually, this limiting of independence is a requirement for the maximum development of human freedom and personality.

Only because of a special kind of freedom does the human being appear in the final stage of evolution as a responsible personality. In man the four main drives are unconscious, but they can become conscious in his judgment and decision. Through creative actions that have meaning in terms of his higher goal, man's original upward tendency achieves its highest quality of existence. This tendency forces us, again and again, to search beyond ourselves for a higher final meaning in our lives. But our search depends, in large part, upon a social organism which is well directed also toward a final goal. The modern ideological pressure for a just world order originates in this primary drive toward higher completion. This evolutionary drive must not be forced backward by counter-evolutionary tendencies of fear or egoistic obstinacy. It must either find its proper goal and meaning or, if it fails, it will destroy the world.

Thus, it is surely one of the basic causes of all revolutions that those who start them see in existing society no hope for becoming a higher goal-oriented community. Nor do these revolutionaries find in society the ideals to satisfy their deepest human need: their longing for meaning in life. When, therefore, a generation undertakes social revolution, releasing the "aggressive drive" and discarding inhibitions meant to control all inner drives, the result is a wrong orientation in these drives.

The loss of normally present restraints leads to self-destruction. The hunger drive and the urge to acquire possessions run off the track, as it were, into an economic race that ruins all higher efforts. The sex drive "loses its head." The drive to escape is expressed in flight from responsibility, flight from risks, flight from decision. Naked fear and cowardice are covered with the cloak of love for peace. Pacifism can be as self-destructive as the uncontrolled aggressive drive that was so impelled by hatred in Germany's socialistic past.

The evil resulting from loss of restraint in the drives is apparent today. We see the destruction that results from disoriented self-seeking, along with abandonment of the common good. Because we offer only the consumption of sex and material things along with flight from responsibility, the young generation, which strongly searches for high ideals, naturally tends toward revolution. Also, in our present situation, we can see the schizophrenia of talking about "democracy" and "collegiality" while forming endless bureaucracies that bury individual creativity and responsibility.

The "Will Toward Meaning" and Man's Instinctive Drives

Konrad Lorenz, in writing about the four basic drives in nature — the hunger, sex, aggressive and escape drives — proves that they are a main requirement for the evolution and the preservation of life. The hunger drive which makes the hamster prepare for winter is also a very natural source of evolution for man. He needs this drive for his own preservation and development. The same is true, of course, for the other drives. The sex drive increases the species. The aggressive drive defends the species against everything which destroys life. And when the organism senses danger, the escape drive causes it to react instinctively with flight. The respective drives express themselves not only in hunger, thirst, sex, and so on, but also in feelings of inferiority, hatred, longing, fear, etc. Satisfying these drives changes desire to pleasure.

Man, as a questioning, reflecting, reminiscing being, has the capacity for following the directions of reason. But whenever he tries to order his drives and energies to a higher meaning, he feels a tension between his instinctive drives and his reason. The less a person has learned to think and reflect, the sooner the pleasures of life deriving from the basic drives will suffice for him. A good meal satisfies the hunger drive. Fulfilled sexuality causes pleasure. A political, military, scientific, cultural or moral victory satisfies the aggressive instinct and results in a goodly sense of gratification. Also, escaping from danger results in feelings of relief and satisfaction.

There seems to be a question as to whether the human being obeys his drives to have pleasure or whether these drives, including the desire for pleasure, are simply hereditary patterns of behavior ordered toward a general goal. We need not resolve this question here. But there are many examples of individual and social disaster resulting from a wrong ordering of our basic drives.

In 1945, when peace seemed to be the most important common good in the atomic age, and when the human aggressive drive was held responsible for the Second World War, it was suggested that this drive should be killed in the "aggressive" Germans. The idea was to re-program the German people so that their energies could be channelled into the other drives. The so-called peace research attempt resulted in a study of the aggressive drive in order to find ways to overcome, minimize, or control this drive.

Since human beings have only a certain amount of energy available for the fulfillment of various instincts, it was suggested that all thought and effort should be concentrated on the satisfaction of the other three drives, thus permitting the aggressive drive to deteriorate. This was done with psychological finesse through a program of "re-education" of the German people. The familiar, popular, national, and religious values from which the aggressive drive gets its energy were systematically played down and made to seem devilish and ridiculous. It was intended that this drive would express itself, at most, in sports. Family traditions, interest in ancestors, as well as the sense of belonging to a family, etc., which had formerly been so important to the people, were repressed. Television and films no longer showed the positive political, cultural, scientific and religious role of Germany in the development of Europe and the modern world. In order to give youth a repugnance for their own nation, only concentration camp, criminal, western and sex films were shown. As a result, Christian youth sing the national anthem with ridicule, even to this day.

History classes in schools also were changed. Karl Marx became more important than Martin Luther or any other really important person in German history. The wars of defense in the last centuries, and even those against the Huns, Arabs, Hungarians, Turks, Slavs and French, were lumped together with the last two wars declared by the Germans, thus putting still more blame on Germany and declaring all we did a catastrophe. The soldier, the image of manliness, ready to sacrifice his life for his country, was ridiculed and replaced by the image of women, pacifistic cowards and inane heroes.

All energy was channelled into satisfying the hunger drive and the drive to acquire material things. After the worst part of the destruction left by the war was cleaned up, human energy was increasingly used for the production of sexual pleasure, which was isolated from its creative task. In the absence of any higher ideal, the escape drive was expressed in political, military and moral pacifism; it turned people away from every type of genuine and challenging responsibility.

The discarding of the aggressive drive, along with higher ideals pertaining to the common good, naturally resulted in the inability of the other three drives to be directed toward higher meaning or to be guided by a superior control. Thus, these drives, which are normally meant to serve the preservation of the species, were perverted. Being wholly directed toward achieving the greatest possible satisfaction and pleasure, they became diseased. These drives automatically became counter-evolutionary forces, destroying both individual persons and the community.

The hunger drive became not only a gluttonous desire to eat and drink, with all its bodily and psychological consequences, but also a destroyer of the economy. The greed of workers could no longer be distinguished from that of employers, officials, teachers, doctors, or pastors. With an increase in laziness, dishonesty, exploitation of the state (which in turn deceived individual citizens), etc., a situation developed in the country which had to result in inflation, strikes, unemployment, and finally, in hunger, misery, revolution and confusion.

The same was true of the sex drive. When it became uninhibited and autonomous, this drive no longer served its proper purpose, that is, the creation of new life. Without a higher goal or meaning, this drive turns against human beings and society, destroying both. It acts like the uninhibited energy of the cancer cell; after it loses its guiding image in the nucleus and the higher purpose of the cell's existence, this energy becomes "malicious." Similarly, the results of a wrongly directed, autonomous sex drive are premature exposure of children to sex and the destruction of the family. This drive shows its life-destroying effect not only in the "anti-baby pills" but also in the killing of the unborn — all for the sake of having sexual pleasure without the "danger of a child."

The uninhibited escape drive shows itself in a growing blindness toward actual situations. It resists the development of responsibility in normal citizens. Many anonymous letters, indicating harmless needs, were sent to professionals in previous years because the writers were afraid! How disturbing are cowardice and irresponsibility, especially in Christian politicians! How quickly most of them capitulate because of fear, criminality, wrong political ideas and economic theories which threaten to destroy everything!

Even the army and police are beginning to capitulate. The democratic process seems to be moving in the direction of reducing genuine responsibility in the state, in business, in the schools, and in the family. Flight to the complete protection of the community makes all genuine responsibility impossible. Indeed, it is socialistic communism, with its counter-evolutionary force, that takes such responsibility to itself and discards private ownership by trying to kill the hunger drive and the drive to acquire. These drives actually are declared by the state to be evil.

On the other hand, as a result of Manichean influences, there were efforts in the Church to condemn sex as evil and to suppress its normal expression, instead of giving the sex drive its proper direction and control.

Previously, through systematic political education, national Socialism had tried to suppress the escape drive and to mobilize the aggressive drive along with the ideal of hero-worship. This exacted of the German people a great price and almost resulted in the annihilation of our country.

From what has been said we can draw the following conclusions:

1. Because man is a thinking, questioning being, he has the capacity to control, sublimate and re-program his instincts.
2. Man also can choose the opposite of meaning in life and make the pleasures of his basic drives his goal, thus changing these drives into a counter-evolutionary force.
3. Since the basic drives are important to life, the effort to suppress them is a disastrous mistake that results in a counter-evolution. Therefore, the socialistic attempt to bury the drive to acquire possessions is just as wrong as the Manichean attempt to suppress the sex drive. It is equally wrong to suppress the aggressive drive. And a liberal consumer society which fails to encourage a healthy escape drive, while encouraging an exaggerated aggressive drive, is likewise destructive.
4. Because man has the power to reflect on his drives and to influence them, and because he can decide between evolution and counter-evolution, between pleasure at the service of life and pleasure at the service of itself, he is the only being that can pervert all four drives. He is the only living creature that can use his drives for his own annihilation rather than for the preservation and development of life.

The so-called evils are not the instincts or drives themselves, which are so necessary for life, but their perversion by man, who, if he chooses to do so, can make them instruments of evil.

"Will to Pleasure" as an Inversion of the Meaning of Human Instincts

The inner pleasure accompanying every genuine fulfillment of our drives must remain as such. If these drives and instincts are to be successfully integrated within the higher purpose of the total person, the pleasure associated with their fulfillment is necessary.

But when the pleasure and joy connected with the fulfillment of an evolutionary task is used and proclaimed for its own sake, the tendency toward evil is always present. When the will to pleasure replaces the God-given meaning of a drive, that drive becomes a passion; it becomes diseased.

Instead of serving the cause of eating, drinking and doing honest work, the hunger drive is perverted into a gluttonous eating and drinking, into uninhibited greed and exploitation of others.

The sex drive, which is supposed to foster the love and community of two people and their establishment of a family, deteriorates into a passion for sexual pleasure. Instead of forming a family, this perverted drive, with all its degenerative consequences, destroys the family and community.

The aggressive drive, when it is perverted, no longer directs itself against evil; nor does it engage its energy in achieving the high ideals of the community. Instead, it impels a desire for power, position and social prestige. It causes hatred for all that impedes attainment of these goals. And finally it becomes a demon that seeks to destroy the world.

Similarly, the escape drive degenerates into neurotic anxiety or a completely irresponsible cowardice, to the point of suicide. It is, indeed, a flight from life itself.

Perversion of the drives and instincts becomes automatic in a human being when his life as a whole no longer has a higher meaning in which to integrate these instincts. In this regard, there is a fundamental difference between man and animal. Man can choose his goal. Consciously, he can develop his instincts and intelligence for a higher good.

Man is able to control his drives, but he is unable to root them out. If he tries to root out his drives, he discards the necessary controls by which one drive moderates the other. Man must consciously integrate his drives within a "will to the highest meaning." The thrust of evolution points this out to him. Such a direction is even present within plants, animals and the physical-chemical realm of nature.

If the four drives are not integrated within a higher meaning, they become passions that pervert "the will to meaning." The passion for power becomes a search for meaning in power and recognition. The passions for sexual satisfaction and for the pleasures of eating, drinking, smoking, using drugs, etc., are expressions of a search for higher meaning through increased pleasure and satisfaction. The passion of greed is also a perversion of the drive for meaning. However, none of these misguided desires can answer our search for real meaning in life. Indeed, by searching in the wrong places, the passion causes an ever-greater "thirst" for meaning. In this way the passion becomes ever more meaningless. "Thirst" is the most difficult desire to satisfy. And "thirst for the living water," that is, for meaning in life, is even stronger than the sex drive, which, in its elementary state, never achieves satisfactory meaningfulness. The meeting of Jesus and the Samaritan woman, who "already had six husbands" and whose present husband "is not your husband either" (John 4:10) is a living illustration of this fact.

If a deep longing for greater meaning in life is found in all that exists, then suppression of this inner longing and failure to find greater meaning must result in frustration, neurosis and illness in human beings.

Logotherapy

Viktor Frankl of Vienna, a famous neurologist and psychiatrist, and the founder of logotherapy, proves that there is a connection between neurosis and a lack of meaning.[2] In doing so, he recognizes that a certain kind of neurotic disturbance cannot be cured by psychotherapy, but can be cured by leading the person, through logotherapy, to a meaning in life. Such disturbances and illnesses, called "noogenic neuroses," because they have their origin in the spiritual part of man, cannot be cured by satisfying the libido.

None of the materialistic philosophers or ideologists can answer satisfactorily the question of meaning in life so as to fill the emptiness of human existence. Marx, Feuerbach, Nietzsche, Sartre, Bense, Marcuse, Reich and others had no valid answer to the deepest longing of man. In this connection, it would be relevant to examine the transition in the evolutionary process that took place in Jesus of Nazareth. Without the help of modern techniques He demonstrated in His "miracles" the control of nature through the spirit. He showed the strength of His "will to meaning" by overcoming death. He overcame fear by willingly going the way of the cross. For many of His friends and disciples, He pointed the way to a previously unknown quality of existence called "eternal life." No one will deny that Jesus, more than anyone else, influenced the past 2000 years of world history.

He did not favor the discarding of ownership, nor did He argue against the sex drive and the other human drives. But He gave each human desire a new goal in a higher meaning. He regarded ownership as a God-given stewardship, which one must administer responsibly in the service of others. He saw the sex drive as an aspect of an indissoluble partnership in the community of marriage. Aggression against evil in the world was seen as an aid to the rule of God. And He integrated the escape drive into a respectful fear of God. How often He said "Do not be afraid," while teaching the subordination of all human desires to an indivisible community with the "Father." This new relationship with the Father He explained in terms of membership within the "body," and branches of the "vine." It would be a worthy study to trace the unique "mutation" in disposition, motivation and behavior that took place in Christ's personal and community life. The results of such a study would strengthen our hypothesis.

Evolution toward Freedom

The way of evolution is one of increasing freedom. The ability to choose a goal of ultimate meaning — communion with God — can come about only through inner freedom.

In his book *Evolution in Action*, Julian Huxley says that, after Hegel, "World history of progress is made with an awareness of freedom." [3] Dr. Paul Campbell, the well-known doctor and scholar of political evolution, begins with the basic facts of evolution in his book *Modernizing Man*.[4] According to Dr. Campbell, the increasing complexity of the brain and nervous system predisposes for a greater disposition of self toward freedom. Higher biological complexity makes possible a greater capacity for adjustment to, and independence from, the limitations of life. In this regard, man is certainly the most highly developed being. He has the ability to react to possibilities, to choose and to decide. Thus, he can reach the greatest exterior and interior independence and freedom; he can rule the world around him, and even can view the earth from the moon.

The decisive requirement for discovering freedom of decision and action as the last known stage of evolution was man's possibility of recognizing higher meanings. Therefore, the way toward developing a free personality in the individual, as well as in the nation, is the ever-new attempt to control the outer and inner limitations of life.

The struggle for freedom takes place on three levels:

1. the struggle for freedom from external threats to human life through the greatest possible independence from hunger, sickness, catastrophes of nature, extremes of weather, intrusions by animals or parasites, etc.;
2. the struggle for freedom from control and exploitation by other men, nations, classes and races;
3. the struggle for inner freedom from the reactions of wrongly directed autonomous drives and the dictatorship of instincts and passions: freedom from fear, greed, hatred, etc.

Whoever fails to achieve inner freedom also will be unable to achieve external freedom.

Without an ordering of inner drives to an ultimate meaning, there can be no inner freedom. The drives then become autonomous and rule the whole man; they become destructive and counter-evolutionary. The same is true for external freedom, without which it is difficult to maintain inner freedom. Without the right to own and to dispose of his own property, a man's inner freedom of decision is in danger of being robbed by the state or the corporation. If the goal of those in power is to exploit people rather than to serve them, any national, unionized or private capitalistic concentration of power increases the danger of exploitation and dictatorship. Any form of capitalistic or communistic exploitation is always counter-evolutionary, a reactionary step backward.

Political freedom is inconceivable without sharing power. But a society that functions by sharing power must value man as something much more than an accidental product of nature. Social order is possible only when laws guarantee the individual the right to life in all stages of his development, and also guarantee his freedom of conscience and decision.

Whether such a free state continues to function is dependent upon the will of its citizens. Are they prepared to defend this type of society? To protect the right to life of all through law? To constantly strengthen inner freedom by subordinating drives and instincts to a higher goal and by striving for a common world order? Whether in the realm of economy, politics, or sex, uncontrolled drives always lead to the inner enslavement and exploitation of others. And the loss of inner freedom leads automatically to the deterioration and loss of exterior freedom. An economy which strives only after gain has no real permanency. The same is true for politics which seek nothing but power, and for sexual relationships which have as their primary or exclusive goal the experience of pleasure. A counter-evolutionary situation has no future.

The Sexual Revolution as Counter-Evolutionary

The capacity of man to decide between evolution and counterevolution, or to direct his main drives either toward their evolutionary meaning or toward pleasure for its own sake, brought about the so-called sex revolution of the past 20 years. This "revolution," because of the elimination of pertinent higher ideals in our modern use-and-discard society, has resulted in the degeneration of the sex drive.

Revolution means turning things upside-down. Impersonal sexual lust, which has departed from "personal love of the sexes," has become the highest value in society. As a result, sexual expression is no longer determined by "knowing" (Adam knew Eve), but by sexual lust. The reasons of the heart (*Les raisons du coeur*: Pascal) have become silent. One could say that the cerebrum gives orders to the medulla, and the latter becomes a mere functionary of the genital organs.

Just as the hunger drive is turned from its proper goal toward the greed of egoistic consumption by the pressure of continual advertizing, so the sexual drive is turned toward lust by the constant advertizing pressures of the sexual revolution. People become sex-greedy.

But we must remember that the decisive difference between human sexuality and that of animals consists in the fact that animal sexuality is directed exclusively by instinct, while human sexuality is designed to be directed by reason. This difference is already apparent in the location of the sex organs in most animals. These organs are located on the same horizontal level as the head. In man, however, the location of the sex organs is vertically far below the brain. This expresses the fact that human sexuality is meant to be controlled by human will and consciousness. For this control, the human being is responsible.

Therefore, man's perversion of his sexual values through a "sexual revolution" leads to behavior below that of animals, where sex organs not only are located horizontally with the brain but are directed by instinct at very definite times of the years. The sex-greedy person, on the other hand, is constantly driven by the dictatorship of a sex drive which has degenerated into passion. Thus, the sex revolution is not concerned with human progress, but with a counter-evolutionary attempt to reverse the development of man.

Sex Education and Counter-Evolution

If one looks at modern literature explaining sex, one must conclude that the writers, as perverts and sexually confused people, make exploitation of others their norm. The situation becomes criminal when teachers of "sex education" or counselors of families give young girls guidance on sexual intercourse and lesbian perversion. Indeed, when one listens for two hours at a meeting of the *Bundestag* to Mr. Kentler, who bears the proud title of "Department Leader at the Pedagogical Center in Berlin" and who, as early as 1967, arranged for sex education of the young, one no longer is surprised on finding a sex primer in which children aged six or seven are given detailed instruction about ways of achieving sexual pleasure.[5] In the meantime, the sex atlas formerly used with fourteen-year-old children has been declared a harmless cultural text.[6] In this atlas, published by the government, every higher human value is denied. Children are taught details about contraceptives as protection against "the danger of a child."

In his book on sex, Mr. Verch from Hamburg teaches that in the first three months of pregnancy, the human being is only a kind of cellular clump, and that it may be removed without a scruple, exactly as a wart or a maw-worm would be removed.[7] In these explanations of sex there is no mystery; nothing is sacred. Truth and reality are violated. Indeed one is pressured to conclude that there are no taboos any longer, because these are dangerous. In such books and films, one gets the impression that all human existence is fully understood and that there are no secrets or mysteries left to be discovered. The average modern man seems to ask fewer questions than the little child.

Because of this flat type of sex education in which only exterior qualities are presented, we are seeing such consequences as uninhibited "ladies" haughtily marching the streets with screaming signs: "My body belongs to me." It seems that the miracle of human existence, beginning with conception, has become a contradictory by-product of sexual pleasure. And it seems that this by-product must be put aside, hindered, and, if necessary, destroyed like a burdensome parasite. No wonder, when the union of cells at conception and the development of life until birth are presented in books that pretend to know everything about the "how" and "why" of this wonderful process! There is nothing anywhere available in which the mystery of the origin of human life and human personality is explained.

It is strange that so many people are satisfied with knowing how two cells unite, then divide into two, four, eight, sixteen, thirty-two cells, etc., as shown in films today. It is strange that the most important questions are never asked. Why is the result of this division not just a heap of cells? Why does the process of division result in a human organism with its amazingly intricate complexity? What is this capacity for organizing, planning and ruling an organism? Such relevant questions are quickly referred to the realm of myth. Modern natural science, by mere external description, dares to imply that the "image" of God is a clump of cells.[8] It dares to insinuate that God is only an extrapolation of human anxieties about the mysterious powers of nature and of death — a "hovering" between nothing and meaning. Is God a wish fulfillment, a product of the imagination?

No! It is certainly stupid to think that we can discover the innermost reality of our existence by filming the exterior events that accompany the origin of man. Indeed, even if we could learn to change our genetic information — a remote possibility — we still would know nothing about the ultimate "why" of our origin and the innermost reality of our being. No physicist, chemist, biologist or geneticist has been able to answer, on a purely scientific basis, the "why" of our existence.

Sex Acceleration in the Child as Counter-Evolutionary

It is counter-evolutionary to say that the child is a "sexual being," instead of saying that the child is a being with sexuality. Whoever, without rose-tinted ideological glasses, observes a child, recognizes that the sexual drives of the very young are minimal in comparison to their need for meaningful affirmation and adaptation to the environment. Satisfaction for a child is in no way sexual pleasure. The little embryo may begin to suck its thumbs as early as the fourth month; but in so doing it is simply training the muscles of its mouth for sucking, necessary for life after birth. The attempt to explain an "oral and anal phase" of sexuality in a child, and to declare thumbsucking, nailbiting, etc., as sexual activity, is entirely arbitrary and has no scientific basis.[9] On the contrary, the child demonstrates the "will to meaning" in a classic way. His longing for motherly love and acceptance has nothing to do with sex satisfaction; it is an expression of the basic drive in all existing beings toward the will to meaning. Sexual lust, gluttony, or other passions are results of frustration in the will to meaning. Bedwetting is in no way an expression of hidden sexuality; it is most often indicative of a faulty relationship of the child with his family or his surrounding environment.

The so-called sex "acceleration," a typical expression, is part of a counter-evolutionary reversal in human development. It means that sexual development begins progressively sooner in the young generation, while character development and spiritual maturation take place much more slowly. Because of sex acceleration, the age of puberty begins on an average of two years earlier, while spiritual development is retarded or remains infantile.

Such a reversal in development causes regression to the level of some mammals with a more primitive brain.* Today we actually plan this reversal of development, programming the counter-evolution of man. Sex texts used by six- or seven-year-old children artificially awaken certain impulses and force them into premature sexual behavior. This is a devilish plan. It is certainly possible to accelerate sexual development, to make children sex-hungry; and it is certainly possible to retard their spiritual and character development, and thus to manage a counter-evolution.†

*An example of such manipulations is the program of sexologist Helmut Kentler, who makes his own abnormality the public norm. In Muehlheim, as the main speaker on the sexuality of children, he demanded that they be exposed to pornography already at age three. †In this connection it is interesting to note the rapid sexual development of caged cow herons, as discovered by the English ethnologist and sociologist Professor I. D. Unwin (*Sex and Culture*, Oxford University Press). His research causes him to affirm the direct connection between the rise of culture and the control of sexual energy, or between cultural decadence and sexual permissiveness.

The political counter-evolution uses sex training of children in kindergartens and schools for the purpose of destroying families and society. This is being done by "psychologists," young teachers, blundering religious instructors, etc. Instead of educating children for a higher meaning in life, which integrates pleasure (not as an end in itself, but as an incentive accompanying creative activity), the "right to pleasure" is everywhere stressed. When one observes the commotion about sex education, and the results, one has to believe either in the insanity of those concerned or in their radical stupidity.

Counter-Evolution in the Husband

Our world has been called "the world without a father." No wonder, the sexual counter-evolution has eliminated the aggressive drive! Lacking a well-ordered aggressive drive, men desire sex without responsibility. They become unmanly and frightened by the thought of having to assume economic responsibility for a family; they instinctively try to escape.

Feeling no responsibility toward his emancipated, pill-taking wife, nor toward his anti-authority children, such a male becomes a moral and political pacifist. He suns himself in the glow of his own love for freedom, which he thinks is being progressive, but which is, usually, only cowardice. He is a Casanova with a sexual performance complex and with hyperactive drives to possess things and to escape from accountability. He cynically tries to hide the infantilism of his character. His life is centered around his sports car, his cigarettes and his own pleasures. He appears to be manly, but shows anger in a group, and cowardice when alone. He has no sense of honor nor any desire to fight. He has nothing left within him but a central control for vegetative reactions.

Naturally, there are many variations to the theme. But it could be frightening to go through the crowds at a festival and to see so many dull faces, and eyes without vision or signs of spiritual development. Two years ago at a dance where nearly one thousand persons had gathered, I noticed many who sat dully on the floor, listening to the loud hammering of musical instruments. I was alarmed at the sight of so many dull faces, faces which reminded me of the stupor in the mentally ill.

This general attitude of many men who lack a positive, well-ordered aggressiveness naturally affects vocational and cultural enterprise. Dynamic personalities, qualities of leadership, authority and creative initiative are becoming more rare. Even in the area of apprenticeship, interest in handwork is decreasing in favor of state office jobs with pensions.

Naturally, the "man" who does not want to be a "father," and certainly not a "grandfather," looks for the type of woman who will accommodate herself to him, a woman whom he can exchange, use or discard, like a cheap coat. He wants to suggest to her that she become emancipated by becoming unstable and unattached, that she fight against the opposite sex, and that she acclaim the right to kill her own prenatal children instead of raising them.

Counter-Evolution in the Wife

The phrase "emancipation of women" is the propaganda slogan with which the female "works out" the sexual counter-evolution. Formerly the poet could say, "Blushing he follows her and her greeting makes him happy." Today she follows him without charm or beauty, dressed slovenly, hair dishevelled, wearing pants, shirt hanging out, her made-up eyes looking flat and joyless. Such women regard shamelessness as emancipation; they discuss sex and the "pill" as casually as the noon meal.

Are such women happier than their grandmothers? Are they more free? Have they more to say? Are they respected and loved? The cosmetic mask of many seems to hide restlessness, disgust with themselves, and the emptiness of an unfulfilled life.

Naturally, the counter-evolutionary male prefers the heavily made-up woman, because this mask excuses him from responsibility. Face to face with a masked woman, he is not held to his word. He lies to her, and she tries to deceive him about her true self. She allows a man to feel that he need not believe her, that he need not take her seriously as a human being, and that she will not, and cannot, obligate herself. Her manner tells a man, "I am at your disposal. You need not fear that anything will be taken seriously." At most, conversation and the pleasure of a passing episode are possible with a masked woman, but certainly no permanent bond. She is a type of prostitute who tries to save at least the little which may remain of her true self.

Women are deceived when they think that the equality of husband and wife demands a wife's rivalry with her husband in his field of special competence. If the wife wants to be manly and the husband womanly, they cease being partners. Because the polarity between them and, as a result, their mutual power to attract are lost, they no longer complement each other.

In typically male activities, woman is inferior. And in typically female activities, man is inferior. It is true that many a female sprinter will outrun some men; still the best runner almost always will be a man. On the other hand, there are many good male nurses, but the best care usually is given by a female nurse. There might be men who keep house and raise children. But, as a rule, the mother is indispensable. Equality is achieved through accomplishment and responsibility. Therefore, proportionate to one's nature, an "emancipation" of women that forces them to imitate men leads to greater dependence and inferiority — not to freedom. This becomes clearest where the question of abortion is concerned.

Instead of working so that abortionists are restricted more severely, many women who feel burdened by protective laws fight against the law as such. In doing so, they dismiss the most important personal support they have; they lose protection against predatory males who, threatening to abandon them, force them to have abortions against their innermost wishes. Thus, women are depersonalized in the worst possible way and "estranged from themselves." They become the sex-slaves of men, playthings used according to mens' moods and desires.

The deep counter-evolution involved in this type of "emancipation" is evident in the perversion of woman's natural scale of values. Such perversion is heard in the repugnant cry, "My body belongs to me!" and in the cynical proclamation of film stars and confused journalists, "I have had an abortion!" Step by step, even in the very sight of her husband, a woman is degraded to a level below the animals. No female animal behaves in such a counter-evolutionary fashion.

Human beings who refuse to recognize their mistakes and correct themselves, who prefer to make their evil conduct the public norm for all, actually lose their right to the joys of human community. Reverence for woman's dignity and her indispensable task of motherhood are basic requirements for genuine societal and human equality.

Women who refuse to follow the plan of development given them by nature end in the spiritual disturbances of a pitiful infantilism. They try to get rid of their inferiority complexes by a desperate effort to impress men and win male approval. But the effort is frustrated because men do not respect the pseudo-manliness and the male-sexual appetite of such women. Thus, the "emancipation" of woman becomes grotesque. She ends as a frustrated old witch who is incapable of community with others and who grows old in hopeless isolation. The sexual emancipation of women is described by George F. Gilder as "sexual suicide" in his book of the same title.[10]

Naturally, a woman can develop her feminine qualities in vocations other than that of being married or having children of her own. She can be a nurse, kindergarten director, social worker, teacher, doctor, theologian, even queen or president. However, these forms of accomplishment were always possible and did not necessarily imply a special emancipation of woman from motherhood. Being a mother is not being a "child-bearing machine." Motherhood is an unconditional "yes" required by woman's greatest vocation and task: the creation, birth, development and education of new life. This vocation is the greatest symbol, ideal and miracle of womanhood; with it Mary, the mother of God, most effectively influenced our Western culture. The attempt to destroy this ideal and to degrade woman to the level of a mere sex partner is the most anti-human urge of the sexual counter-evolution.

Sexual-Socialistic Counter-Evolution

According to the theory of Freud's student Wilhelm Reich, the best way to prepare for a socialistic revolution is to bring about a sexual revolution.[11] This fifty-year-old theory has been stressed in Germany since 1967 by the so-called extra-parliamentary opposition. This social movement forced itself into universities, schools and even into kindergartens, proclaiming a new sexual freedom in the land, battling against "sexual repression," and propagating its confused association of sex and socialism. Thus, in order to get rid of the drive to acquire property, the other drives of sex, aggression, and escape are substituted by being peverted. This is being accomplished by creating a climate of fear and terror, with the help of brain-washing. The attempt to achieve a purely egoistical perversion of the drive toward ownership, in order to thwart the possibility of owning important property used for production such as land and ores, originated in a fundamental mistake made by Marx and Engels. No society has ever endured without private ownership.

Modern behavioral research has proved that even fish have their own areas which they defend with the greatest vehemence. The oldest human skeletons and implements reveal evidence of things that once were regarded as important forms of private property. Every child proves that "mine" and "yours" are ideas existing even before the child can speak.

An attempt to prevent the misuse of ownership by removing the possibility for managing property is like castrating someone in order to prevent the misuse of his sex drive. Such castration produces will-less eunuchs and slaves. In an effort to hinder the extreme possessiveness of a few, the government that takes property away from all suppresses the ownership drive for the purpose of increasing production. But this suppression is a terrible mistake. When men like Stalin, with the help of a functionary social organization, rule all property, they in no way become more selfless or honest than a greedy capitalist. On the contrary, because of their greater power and the absence of competition, they tend more easily to have delusions of greatness; they cause much greater harm.

It is surprising that, even today, half of mankind expects to find paradise on earth. Motivated by absurd expectations, societies attempt to dispose of an important human urge, a fundamental drive which is universally necessary for the development of the species. Interestingly, these untenable dreams and theories appeal to a number of our young students.

The truth about the human ownership drive is, naturally, the same as that about the sex, aggression, and escape drives. Appropriate functioning of all drives is a condition for the evolution of the human being toward freedom. Education is needed to correct their wrong functioning and to direct them well. For this purpose higher goals, which far surpass all material goals, are needed by a society. Correct standards and norms for human drives, as well as the will of people to cooperate with and help each other, also are needed.

Obviously, crude misuse of property should be punished. The expectation that punishment will follow upon abusive behavior gives the escape drive an important chance to function. Fear of the consequences of wrong-doing, such as dismissal or other disadvantages, is a factor without which a normal human community is unable to function. An anti-authority education, on the other hand, violates the escape drive. It is superstitious for educators and politicians to think they can get rid of punishment and lead men on the right way simply by counseling. Sacrificing the escape drive is just as wrong as the opposite attempt to misuse this drive by forcing a certain kind of behavior through pressure and terror. In both extremes, the escape drive turns itself against the evolution of human life toward genuine freedom.

Counter-Evolution in Art

Counter-evolution in a society is the most basic source of all that threatens that society with confusion and degeneration. Today, appealing names are being given to this process of regression. Not only is sexual deterioration being called "revolution," but many forms of unhealthy behavior are being called "progressive." The word "progressive" sounds good; it is filled with futurity. The word "conservative" sounds reactionary.

Unfortunately, the word "progressive" also signifies the process of a disease. Physicians speak of the progressive "disappearance of muscle," or of an advancing "tuberculosis," or of a developing "cancer" or of a progressive "paralysis" and "softening" of the brain. Anyone who wishes to do so is able to call a cancer an interesting appearance of "modern progress" in a bodily organ. One can call it an "emancipated growth of cells," an "anti-authoritarian" condition of cells, or the "freedom of energy to increase within the cells." One could be as excited about a strange form of cancerous growth as my pathology teacher, who, when he pointed out cancer to his students, said, "See, what a wonderful cauliflower cancer!"

Since art, better than anything else, reflects the soul of an age, it is not surprising that some young artists take models from pathology for their sculptures. Mr. Jochen Hiltmann has shown convincingly that in the Federal Republic of Germany the worst trash often is given a prize when it is labeled "progressive." He sculptured in metal a natural-looking pile of elephant manure and called it "sterco d'elephante." And he received prizes from the cities of Baden-Baden, Stuttgart and Mannheim for the best work by a young German sculptor. The director of a museum in another German city was so insulted by Mr. Hiltmann's pathological art that he asked the city council to order an equally natural-looking sculpture of a uterus which had ruptured during an abortion. He urged that the sculpture accurately show the parts of the fetus, and that it be displayed in front of the city's vocational school. Fortunately, a doctor on the city council knew the truth about Hiltmann's sculpture and prevented the progressive city government and its museum director from ordering such a "piece of art," which would have cost 45,000 German Marks. Seen in retrospect, however, it might have been prophetic to have such a sculpture established as a memorial to the "war against the unborn." [12]

Perhaps this example serves to clarify the difference between authentic art and the "art" of the counter-evolution. It shows the cynical misuse of "progressive" art to point out the disintegration of society. It shows the loss of values as demonstrated by pathological content, senseless trash and disgusting perversions. Authentic art would suggest, instead, the ideals of human evolution.

Counter-Evolution in Ideology

As cancer begins with the destruction of the guiding force in the nucleus of the cell, so the destruction of a meaningful ideal affects a nation. An example of this process is the degeneration of a societal ideal in Europe during the last nine hundred years. One would have to write another book to describe it adequately. Here, I would like to sketch briefly this example of counter-evolution.

After 800 A.D., the idea of the Kingdom of God in St. Augustine's *City of God* became the ideal of all Europe. The development of this ideal reached a climax during the reign of Emperor Henry III, who died in 1056, at the age of thirty-nine, in the arms of his best friend, Pope Victor II. His son, Henry IV, and Pope Gregory VII began to destroy this "Kingdom of God" ideal through their efforts to fight and liquidate each other. Both died deposed and banished. But their successors continued the fight for centuries, with the result that the spiritual foundation and political ideal of the "Kingdom of God" were destroyed. After the Pope banished the emperor, and after the penance of Henry IV at Canossa in 1077, unity between Pope and emperor became no more than a pious wish in Christianity. In fact, the result was that *parts* of what remained of the "city of God" were over-emphasized and made absolute.

The lost unity thus became the "highest value," in fact, the most important idol. (The Greek word *eidolon* means false god.) On the other hand, "Roman Catholicism" and "Greek Orthodoxy" became symbols of a divided Christianity. Finally, the protest of conscience against enforced Christian unity led to a proclamation of "conscience" as the highest value. In Protestantism conscience became an idol.

During the religious wars and the Inquisition, many people were killed in the name of an absolute, but partial, ideal. Needing finances to pay for these constant battles, emperors and popes sold their feudal benefices. The result was a changeover from fiefdom to private ownership. Ownership was canonized and made absolute. The previous right to inherit and own became a form of absolutism or capitalism. At the same time the meaning of the family became clear, and family-consciousness influenced economics, politics and culture.

In the so-called Renaissance, a new critical awareness developed. The ego, as opposed to society, became more independent, more self-determined. This ego-centered awareness penetrated all areas of life. Not only the Reformation but also economic revolution ensued. When freedom of the individual became an absolute, when liberalism became supreme, one result was the sacrifice of millions of lives in the French Revolution. Finally, Napoleon put an end to simplistic liberalism and completely eliminated the old ideal of the "city of God" by making nationalism absolute. Again, millions became victims of nationalistic wars.

Next came industrialization and a new class, the working class. Another idol was enthroned: class awareness, with its communistic theory. Once again millions of lives were sacrificed to the partial ideal of "social justice."

In responding to the threat of a communistic revolution, a threat resulting from the unemployment of 1929 and the exploitation following the Versailles Treaty, Hitler appealed to a deep collective unconsciousness in the German people. He appealed to a common race, and created race-consciousness as a basis for his ideology. For the sake of this new theoretical idol, millions lost their lives.

Today, the ideological question of a common order for all humanity has become a major problem. The possibility of world annihilation with the atomic bomb has intensified the need for a common order. The welfare of mankind, without God, is the new absolute. Peace at any price is another idol. These forms of humanism and pacifism are the last remnants of the ancient Kingdom of God ideal, and these, too, will demand the lives of millions. Those who dare to oppose peace without justice are persecuted, even now, as enemies of peace and as cold warriors.

It is interesting that these idols, the perverted bastard ideologies of the old Kingdom of God ideal, have become more and more anti-Christian in character. A counter-evolutionary process has relieved current awareness of its last responsibility, thus making personal and collective egoism the order of the day. We are dealing here with a reversal of the meaning of human life, following a revolt of selfishness against a transcendent destiny and responsibility.

The true road of evolution requires self-restraint, family restraint, national restraint, racial restraint and world restraint. Even the highest community can be egoistical and make itself the standard for all. It, too, can become counter-evolutionary. Even the world community must transcend itself and follow absolute laws, thus establishing a human organism that is able to function responsibly toward a goal.

Millions of human beings have experienced the right order of the human drives for the individual as well as for nations. They know that this right order is possible and needed. The same demand, from all different perspectives, is clear for mankind today. If we do not oppose the counter-evolutionary trends of our time, with a greater and more inclusive vision of wholeness, we will become the victims of wrong directions in wild, dissociated energies. The hour for a final decision is nearing. What this decision means, in terms of the theme of this book, will be considered more specifically in its second and third parts.

The most specific area for consideration will be the human sexual drive and its reference to meaningful goals in human life. This area will be examined in detail. It will then become more clear that the "emancipation" of the drives is counter-evolutionary to the Creator's plan and is a means of separation from God and from other human beings. In other words, such "emancipation" is sinful. And, as St. Paul said, "The wages of sin is death" (Rom. 6:23).

Part Two

Human Sexuality and Its Norms

he human person is called by his particular kind of responsible consciousness to understand human sexuality as a whole, and not as an arbitrary number of partial functions. If one observes human sexuality in its threefold meaning one finds:

    a) the main biological goal is the preservation of the species, a goal toward which, according to Koester and others, all biological occurrences, without exception, are directed; [13]

    b) the inter-personal formation of community through the complete spiritual-bodily-mental union of two persons, who become a new and greater whole;

    c) the joy and pleasure experienced in the ecstasy of love, in the creation of new life, and in the formation of community.

Individual factors in this total complex of meaning may not be separated from the whole without human damage. Excluding the third factor — love, joy and creative ecstasy — from the whole complex degrades sexuality to the level of manipulated passion, a kind of rape, and destroys community even in marriage. Sexual union is not to be regarded as a "marital duty"; such degrades the partner and destroys marriage in its innermost being.

Similarly, the exclusion of the second factor, the life-long union of two persons, destroys the totality of human sexuality. Begetting a child because of infatuation and sexual desire, without the will to retain a life-long faithfulness of partners and communal responsibility for the child, destroys the trinitarian totality of human sexuality.

Also the attempt to isolate bodily joy, nudity, ecstasy and pleasure from the communal and creative aspects of human sexuality results in a degeneration of the whole. The rise of sex crime, along with increasing use of pornography, proves the inner connection of sex with the family. Isolated "love," beauty, ecstasy and pleasure on the other hand are very quickly perverted into lewdness and passion, the result becoming a vicious circle that reduces partners to things. Urged by the mass media, one partner desires more and more satisfaction, so that the other finally is degraded to a "type."

If one seriously observes the modern sex drive, as it appears on the streets, during vacations, at dances, in the media, etc., one fails to find genuine joy. One can plainly see the absence of that beauty which accompanies the creation of life in all of nature. The loveliness of flowering blossoms before fertilization, the splendor of many animals during their mating season, the song of birds — all express the joy, beauty and ecstasy of the creation of new life.

But the brutalized and mechanized sex drive in our "free" world today discards the ancient rites which even animals had developed, and excludes the whole eros of wooing and love play, in the best sense of the word, in favor of pleasure that is isolated from the true meaning of sex. This whole ugly, joyless development is the offspring of the new technological devices for isolating sexual satisfaction from the creative and communal functions of human sexuality.

Premarital Sex

In an article printed in an Austrian medical journal in 1965, the Viennese psychiatrist Professor Viktor Frankl wrote that love is a relationship between one human being and another which prepares one to become aware of the other in his total individuality and uniqueness. Based on this deep mutual character of love, sexual love has an exclusiveness and permanence that constitute a monogamous relationship.

A sexual union that lacks personal exclusiveness and permanence cannot be called "love." A man who does not offer a woman the assurance of being completely one with him in return for her surrender to him does not love her, but uses her for his own pleasure. Without legal and economic unity, without the public obligation of a relationship's exclusiveness and permanence in marriage, sex always debases woman.

One may say that the clearest evidence of love a man can show a woman before marriage is that he puts his sexuality completely under the control of his responsibility for his beloved. Love shows itself in the will to forgo sex. A man's selfishness and lack of love, on the contrary, appear nowhere stronger than when he desires what is "best for himself" rather than what is best for the woman concerned. He wants her entirely, without giving himself to her completely, that is, without providing legal and economic security.

The time before marriage is a time for integrating sex into personality and placing it under the control of love. Whoever cannot control his sexuality before marriage will be much less able to do so in wedlock, when life is much more intimate. What is not learned regarding sex control before marriage is not learned afterwards either. According to the findings of Kinsey, marriages preceded by sexual involvement ended more quickly in divorce than those of partners who learned sexual control before marriage.[14]

Whenever the sexual act fails to be an expression of complete love, which desires nothing for itself that could harm the partner, it is mere satisfaction of pleasure. This act reinforces an adolescent condition; it does not help to develop the adult kind of love which supports, and sometimes endures, the other for life. In an adolescent, marriage is usually no more than a sex-consumptive relationship which can lay no wholesome claim to exclusiveness and permanence. Often, such a marriage ends in a very short time.

Adult love is unthinkable without a sense of shame. Shameless human beings cannot love in a sensitive and permanent way. They lack esteem for the dignity of another. Those who believe that a sense of shame must be consciously dispelled disturb their own human development and become incapable of love.

In the article mentioned above, Viktor Frankl refers to the modern tendency toward nudity by saying that it is not important whether the top or bottom is exposed, or whether top *and* bottom are exposed. What is important is the fact that the person's face is degraded. The face expresses the sensitive and the human in a person.

Since love is a specifically human aspect of a human being, sexuality deprived of love leads to progressive "depersonalization." A woman who exposes herself to view like a cow in the cattle market, offering her body to everyone's assessing gaze, is generally incapable of adult love which gives all to a single man. A mature woman would not permit hundreds to possess her body in *any* way.

These are not prudish or narrow-minded ideas but logical conclusions derived from the reality of mature love, which must be the goal of all human sexuality.

Premarital sex, then, is a sign of emotional and spiritual immaturity. It is not a sign of anything reasonable or mature. Usually a woman knows that she has surrendered herself for a cheaper price than what she should have demanded as a human being. Her self-awareness is deeply affected by it, and in most cases a phase of depression follows. Many women suffer inferiority feelings and attach themselves to the man on whom they became dependent prematurely. The more the young woman urges marriage (fearing that the man might no longer want her because her worth is lessened), the more the man is repulsed. He found that she lacked the resistance of integrity, and now he is not interested in further conquests. Suddenly she is no longer "understood" by him; there is a quarrel and eventually a separation.

The young woman, now deeply disappointed, tries to compensate for what is lost. She "falls" for the first man she meets who tells her he loves her, so as to experience some worth in spite of herself. This second relationship is even shorter than the first, and disappointment results more quickly. The possibility remains that she might react by "taking revenge" on "men" and "woman," or on society in some way. Her disappointment and inability to find love can lead to complete promiscuity and prostitution. The woman then finds satisfaction in debasing men.

Many wonder whether it might be necessary for the young to learn to know each other sexually before marriage in order to discover whether or not they are compatible. But this is often the surest way to disappointment. Sexual experimenting is not the result of love but of personal selfishness. As a matter of fact, marriage offers the ideal situation for learning to know the other in the total experience resulting from complete surrender to the beloved. The more one wants to experiment to see whether sex will "work out," or is concerned about having pleasure, the more pleasure disappears for him, says Viktor Frankl in *Psychosexuelle Stoerungen*.[15] Fear that sex might not "work out," a bad conscience and inappropriate circumstances attending the sexual act — all these make the probability that it will "work out" very small for a person who cherishes values and discrimination. Concentration on the sexual experience is the surest way to aggravate psychosexual disturbances.

On the other hand, a more wholesome attitude toward sex and marriage results in happiness even if there are problems with sex at the beginning of marriage. A woman once wrote to me:

> I have been married happily for fifteen years. During the first years of our marriage things did not work out sexually at all, but that did not matter to us. If we had "experimented" sexually before marriage, we would very likely have separated and our singularly happy marriage would never have come to be. Only in the course of our life together could we find mutuality in our intimate life and now, as we are getting older, we often say, 'It has never been so beautiful before.' If people love each other deeply, they can do much to make their marriage happy. It always depends on discovering what makes the partner happy. How terribly our young people are being deceived today! They will never come to a happy sexual union formed by love through the much-publicized promiscuous change of partners. The young woman is always the one who bears the brunt, for in women every emotional experience is deeper. Disgust and vexation are the necessary results of promiscuity. I really am not surprised that our young people revert to drugs.
>
> My husband suffered a serious illness in connection with his genital organs, naturally not a venereal disease. For years we could not have sexual intercourse. However, it never occurred to me to find satisfaction elsewhere. A time of sexual continency has never harmed anyone. Quite the contrary. Our parents knew this, too, and they were in no way prudish or narrow-minded, as some like to call them today.

The attitude of "experimenting" with and manipulating one's partner for sexual pleasure, whether in or before marriage, often leads to mutual disgust and contempt. This exploitation-attitude tends to kill love. Because use of contraceptives facilitates sexual exploitation, anyone who accepts contraception for the sake of sexual pleasure loses the opportunity of recommending premarital chastity to young people. There is no essential difference between premarital and marital "emancipation" of sex from its creative purpose. Both are a disturbance of the sex drive in the evolution of personality. Both affect the integration of sex with love, because sex is desired more than the good of the other person. According to Viktor Frankl, only the *I* who loves a *thou* can integrate the *it*.

In conclusion:

1. Premarital sex is always wrong, even when partners later marry, because it is an anticipation of the total bodily union without legal and economic unity. It is not "two in one flesh" in the whole sense of Biblical meaning. This type of sex really occurs with the reservation that the relationship could be dissolved at any time without any problem. However, human sexual love is a singular reality founded on a union of exclusiveness and permanence. Anything less is not authentic love.

2. The singularity of the relationship between man and wife is expressed bodily by the difference between virgin and wife — a difference found only in human beings and regarded by all peoples as important.

3. Premarital sex is not ready to give a child full familial protection. Thus, it regards the child as a problem, and cannot be complete. It tries to achieve temporary sterilization in the woman by any possible means.

4. According to evidence seen in the primitive cultural development of the manistic peoples, premarital sex as a societal practice is a sign of cultural degeneration. Theistic cultures, that is, higher cultures with faith in God, all have premarital continence as a principle of behavior.

5. From the standpoint of Christian faith, premarital sex is a gross offense against the divine order and commandments. It is, therefore, a separation from God, or a grave sin. Its consequences are: loss of higher meaningfulness, destruction of the family, rise of divorces, ambition, mistrust, inability to rear children, political radicalism, anarchy and revolution.

6. Resignation to the situation is not a solution to the problem, even though the majority of young people act as if premarital sex were their natural right, and even though they regard those who practice purity and continence as stupid. These qualities are decisive for personality development and the ability to love. Their absence, as in the case of the prodigal son, never can satisfy human beings. Hunger and thirst for a really meaningful life are never satisfied by sexual pleasure, drugs, alcohol, etc. On the contrary, they are increased.

The most important question to the older generation is whether there are fathers and mothers who can believe in a "return home" for the young generation, as the prodigal son did when he said, "I will break away and return to my father and say to him, 'Father, I have sinned against God and against you. I no longer deserve to be called your son. Treat me as one of your hired hands!" (Luke 15:18).

The experience of forgiveness and the healing of guilt through complete honesty and the resolution to improve is open to everyone. Many Christians, such as St. Augustine, experienced forgiveness and purification through the blood of Christ. Jesus himself asked the woman caught in adultery whether or not anyone had condemned her. When she replied that no one had done so, Jesus said to her, "Neither do I condemn you. You may go. But from now on avoid this sin" (John 8:11).

Keeping in mind the necessity for balancing the three areas of meaning in human sexuality in all questions about moral behavior, we can better consider the reasons why the old sex morality is failing today, and why a new sex morality with absolute norms is needed.

The Old Sex Morality No Longer Adequate

In our world today, it is not sufficient to derive human behavioral norms and laws solely from the knowledge of religious revelation. Such norms cannot make binding demands on a pluralistic society. Behavioral norms also must be derived from scientific knowledge.

The fact that many different "morals" and "customs" are found in various cultures seems, at first, to exclude any common moral laws that would be valid for everyone. But cultural variety is too quickly being interpreted to mean that there is no moral law at all. Thus, the old sex morality is too quickly discarded and not replaced with better behavioral norms. The result is the present chaos of lawlessness, the sexual counter-evolution. Substituting total freedom for clear behavioral norms in personal "conscience decisions" is naive and irrational. How can "conscience" be capable of functioning properly without clear standards and corresponding ethical and religious education?

The old sexual morality generally was rooted in an agrarian economy. Before industrialization took place, there was no extensive need for family planning or birth control. A certain form of family planning did exist in the framework of customary usage, but it was not known as such by the masses. Because of the higher rate of infant mortality and a shorter life expectancy, a larger number of births was necessary to keep the population constant. Thus, for example, the large number of children in farm communities was considered a special blessing from God. Children were the cheapest labor. Even today, in developing agrarian countries, a large family is considered a sign of prosperity.

Formerly, in Europe, only the oldest son and some of the daughters on the farm became married. The other members of the family often stayed on as single hired hands. Some entered monasteries; others became soldiers, emigrated or developed a trade. Obviously this custom made a rapid increase in population impossible. At the same time, there were many deaths because of illness or disease. Even for marriage the sexual motive usually was not decisive. The first consideration was the continuation of a task in progress in a family.

Furthermore, the teaching of St. Paul that "marriage is good" but "remaining single is better" was a societal axiom. This encouraged the single way of life. The unmarried received full recognition and were given equal status with the married in human society. In religions such as Buddhism and Christianity, the religiously motivated unmarried state was long considered the higher of the two states. For the married, on the other hand, the biblical challenge, "Be fruitful and increase; fill the earth and subdue it," was considered a divine and civic duty toward the state.

Modern scientific progress, with its technological and industrial development, completely changed that situation. Infant mortality, puerperal fever, complications at birth, epidemics and the death rate of adults have decreased so rapidly that the average life expectancy has doubled. Simultaneously, due to the use of contraceptives, the birth rate among white peoples has decreased so much that some highly industrialized nations must now import thousands of guest workers because they do not have sufficient laborers of their own. The policy of legalized abortion upon request, advocated by some political parties and promoted in many countries, very likely will lead to genocide in Western European nations.

Another problem with the old sex morality was that it was bound up with traditions that did not consider husband and wife morally and legally equal. For example, the woman was more severely punished than the man for adultery or loose premarital sexual conduct. The law even demanded that she "could never evade her marital duty." A rather characteristic English law, which was enforced until recently, forbade the husband to whip his wife in the evening between seven and ten o'clock, lest the neighbors be disturbed by the wife's loud cries!

Even religion made some general demands: that one love and honor one's partner, that the wife be subject to her husband, that the marriage partners not interfere with the nature of the sexual act and that partners not deprive or be excessive with each other. Society demanded an appropriate marriage and a good premarital reputation on the part of the bride. The husband, however, could "sow his wild oats" before marriage.

The American statistician M. L. Terman shows how far removed modern society is from the old morality.[16] In 1907, ninety out of a hundred brides, and fifty percent of all husbands, were virgins at the time of marriage. Since then this percentage has declined to such a point that virginity is the rare exception.

The Prevention of Ovulation and the "Right to a Happy Sex Life"

The old sex morality received its strongest blow through the introduction of modern contraceptives, specifically those chemicals that prevent ovulation. With this technique the old idea that one may not change the nature of the sexual act was simply and conveniently bypassed. Since the medications used to prevent ovulation also were used to correct irregularity and sterility in women, the transition from "natural" to "artificial" became more vague. It was easy, then, to rationalize the use of these medications for birth control. In a civilization made artificial by man, the question regarding real "nature" becomes more and more problematic.

Along with the possibility of isolating sexual pleasure from its creative task of forming the community, the barriers against premarital sex were lifted. It no longer seemed necessary to reserve sexual union for marriage, since the tie of sexual union with the birth of a child could now be broken. If, within marriage, sexual pleasure may be contraceptively isolated from the possibility of new life, there seems to be, according to many, no sensible reason why premarital sex should be forbidden.

According to the most recent mentality, then, it is expecting too much of unmarried persons that they forgo this "great pleasure." If everyone has a guaranteed right to a "happy sexual life," and if the population explosion demands an isolation of this sexual activity from the possibility of a child, encouraged by the assistance of publicly financed anti-baby counseling, then there is no apparent societal, legal or moral barrier against premarital sexual happiness.

Because of the justifying implications for themselves and for their own perverted "happy sex life," it is not surprising that homosexuals fought so hard for the free use of the "pill." Chemical contraception, in a similar way, has reinforced self-justifications for lesbianism, sodomy, masochism, masturbation, group sex, pornography and other sexual perversions.

The Decadent Re-evaluation of Masturbation

It is significant that with the "emancipation" and isolation of sexual pleasure from the totality of human sexuality, masturbation has been completely re-evaluated.

In human sexuality, the structure of the human body and its organs are designed for the partner. By its very nature the sexual structure embodies and symbolizes the total unity of man and wife in a most intimate union for the purpose of forming a new person. Therefore, one cannot deny that sexuality which is directed *only* toward self-gratification is radically disoriented and perverted.

In spite of this, masturbation is no longer regarded as sinful by "new theologians" or by the "Dutch Catechism." [17] Indeed, there are numerous modern books and atlases on sex which systematically discuss masturbation and encourage children to use it at an early age. Every child perceives at once its essential wrongness, and the question as to whether it is sinful, or separates one from God, cannot be left to "progressive" theologians. There are, doubtless, many young persons who never were educated as to what masturbation is or that it is sinful, yet who, nevertheless, experienced that this type of sexual pleasure is wrong. They intuitively sense that their relationship with God — which is experienced in dialogue, in listening and obeying, in reverence and humility before the Creator of all things — is disturbed through such misuse of a creative gift. Therefore, theological judgment must be made about the central question of man's relationship with God. Such a theological judgment presupposes that the theologians themselves have experienced God's existence as a constant reality in life. But this is certainly not true of many theologians today, because of their own "sexual emancipation."

It is a fact that educators, especially Christian educators, instead of really helping youth, actually lead them to self-abuse by threats, black-mailing, etc. This happens naturally, also, by awakening a conscious need, as is often done by modern "educators." In either case, masturbation can become a passion which actually leads to considerable harm in the development of the nervous system and of personality. The inner isolation and frustration which often cause this abuse are deepened, forming a vicious circle, which ultimately can lead to psychosis.

As with all human problems, freeing a person from a habit of self-abuse demands that the situation be neither minimized nor dramatized. Certainly, there must be no artificial awakening of need; instead the person concerned must be helped by finding in his life a higher meaning, and by an honest confession of guilt and receiving forgiveness. As with learning to ski, the beginner often falls. But the more he learns to control body and skis, the less frequently he falls. No one would say that falling is "necessary" or "right." It is, and remains, a mistake, and real satisfaction is felt only when that mistake is overcome.

Learning to control one's drives, discovering their real meaning, and integrating them into one's personality demands an "apprenticeship," which is required also for human sexuality. Masturbation, petting and premarital sex are not good introductions to a meaningful sexuality, but are symptoms of an inability to properly integrate sex and personality. These activities are like eating the dough before the cake is baked. One can assume that young people who do not learn to control their sexuality before marriage are incapable of the mature love and partnership which presuppose self-restraint and control of the sex drive.

Talk about "the practice of sex" and "the need for masturbation" originates with those who never learned to control their own sex drive, or who would like to justify their own sexual perversion and make it a public norm. Among some primitive peoples, onanists are despised and admonished by the elders.[16] To whom would it occur to consider thumb-sucking or nail-biting as a "necessary phase of development" or an "introduction to eating and drinking"? Or who would call lying and stealing normal because most children and some adults have lied or stolen? But modern sex educators reason in this distorted way about sex. Orgasm seems to be their only goal. They strive to normalize contraceptives, sexual techniques and sex perversions, thus making millions sex-hungry, and ultimately separating many people from society and from God. For many couples, the relationship before and after marriage becomes one of mutual masturbation. In such a relationship, partners misuse their creative energies for their own self-centered satisfaction and pleasure. Instead of loving each other, they become miserable and frustrated.

The Effect of the "Pill" upon Premarital Chastity

In an article in *Stimmen der Zeit*, 1967, the moral theologian Professor Boeckle denied that the acceptance of contraceptives for married couples would make it difficult for the Pope to expect chastity from the young.[18] Very likely he has noticed since then that this was wishful thinking. Most young Christian people re-acted to the exploding propaganda for anti-baby "pills" in a way quite opposite to Professor Boeckle's expectation. They reacted exactly as had been predicted ten years ago in the statement made by the medical doctors of Ulm.[19] These young people now regard anti-procreative sex as the "democratic right" of all citizens whether married or not. They think that one may choose to forgo sex activity if one wishes to become a Catholic priest, or if one has some personal or religious inhibitions. However, in no case may one deny this "happiness" to anyone who uses sex for "love," or for an ideological, political reason, and who, therefore, thinks he can reconcile it with his "conscience." According to the notion of the "critical" young, everything that can be discussed is there-by permitted.

Tolerance Toward Malignancy Is Part of That Malignancy

The ideology of tolerance in dialogue has an unhappy effect as well as one that is beneficial. Moral pacifism has begotten the mistaken notion that one must co-exist in "tolerance" and "dia-logue" with *all* the negative developments of our time. Instead, one ought to strongly resist conduct which destroys human beings and rots the human community to the core. An example of this type of destructive conduct is the programmed perversion of chil-dren through sex education that arouses sexual passion for its own sake. One ought to fight this "malignancy" as one would fight can-cer, with all possible remedies.

Cancer develops in an organism when healthy cells begin to tolerate the presence of malignant cells. Cancer cells can form in almost all organisms, but these cells cannot survive as long as surrounding healthy cells do not permit the cancer cells to grow. Tolerance is never appropriate in the face of malignancy! Today, however, moral malignancy is tolerated and pampered, and this tolerance is part of the malignant condition.

Correctly diagnosing the threat of moral malignancy, the Ulm medical doctors, ten years ago, spoke out against public sex education and said that the state has the responsibility to isolate and disinfect the infected whenever a disease breaks out. What would happen if we did not isolate those with a contagious disease, but would diligently foster "dialogue" with them because they cannot help being sick?

Modern sexuality is not a "natural" phenomenon but an infectious moral illness of society. It breaks up families and destroys cultures. This sounds "fascistic," "communistic," "maoistic." It even sounds "Jewish" in the sense that the Hebrew prophets did not "dialogue" with the sex cult of their times. By not doing so, they preserved the existence and culture of the Jewish people for more than three thousand years.

Today most people swim with the current. One is reminded of the adage: dead fish swim with the current; living fish swim against it.

Modern Sexuality as an Artificial Product

A number of so-called "scientific" psychologists, psychotherapists, sociologists, theologians and teachers today assert that the modern "sex revolution" is an expression of natural human drives freed from false taboos and archaic moral laws. But, in the past ten years, increased psycho-biological sexuality has hastened human sexual maturity to such an extent that it is running two or three years ahead of sexual maturity in animals. In all other areas, humans naturally take longer to mature than animals.

As a consequence of forced growth in human sexuality, infantilism lasts longer and spiritual maturity often remains rudimentary. A discrepancy, greater than ever, exists between the emergence of the sex drive and the strength of character needed to integrate it properly into human personality. Whoever believes he can solve this problem through education in sex techniques and contraceptives, with the help of sex atlases and books, has a naïve fetish for sex education, even though he is a member of the federal ministry of health.

In any event, a counter-evolutionary reversal in physical development is paralleled in a counter-evolutionary reversal in spiritual-moral development. And there is a great danger of accelerating this process of reversal by over-stimulating the young. The less decisive and mature of character young people are, the less they will be able to integrate the sex drive, and the sooner they will become sexually autonomous and schizoid. Premature stimulation of the sex drive causes the young person to become a functionary of that drive, instead of a free personality who has learned to control and integrate his drives.

"Degeneration Caused by Affluence" as Seen in the Premature Sex Development of Animals

By withdrawing the risks connected with normal animal survival or by producing a condition of "affluence," premature sex development and the resultant degeneration of the animal may be seen. The Viennese behaviorist Otto Koenig noticed this phenomenon in the cow heron. An especially adventurous bird, this heron is particularly suited for research because it crossed the Atlantic and other oceans, is found in all lands, and is very adaptable. In an experiment, some of these birds were held in a large cage in which they could fly about freely. Since everything was supplied for them, they had no need to hunt for food or for nesting materials. As a result, they degenerated because of their "affluence."

In its normal, natural condition the cow heron develops brooding feathers and becomes sexually mature only when it is two years old. In "affluent" captivity this happened already at the age of one year. All signs of degeneration which we observe in our own affluent society also appeared in these birds. While they lived in strict monogamy in their natural environment, they no longer did so in captivity. Instead they became completely promiscuous, even incestuous. However, in spite of their greater sexual activity, they had a decline in births. The young remained infantile and dependent, permitting older birds to feed them even after they themselves had young of their own. Regretfully, too many modern grandfathers put up with a similar situation. (*See Appéndix II*)

Forms of sexual degeneration also appear in domesticated animals which experience a life of "social security" and "affluence" and need to take no risks for their survival.

Human sexuality can be awakened and excited before and after puberty by constant stimulation. Indeed, attempts to produce or check reactions and instinctive responses through electrical stimuli on the brain or the spinal cord help us to see that the constant stimulation of a drive in the human being leads to a more rapid development of the organs involved. Uninterrupted sex propaganda artificially stimulates a need for sex and influences the entire development of human sexuality in a degenerative way.

A human being can develop every natural drive into a compulsive passion, and, in this way, can cultivate all types of perversions. Similarly, he can control and direct his drives through conscious determination. Indeed, he can also permit them to deteriorate. For example, an unused muscle becomes flabby. On the other hand, constant stimulation and excitation result in premature development, over-development and rapid degeneration.

In his book *Modernizing Man*, Dr. Paul Campbell writes about the psychological connection of human emotions with the hormone glands (hypophesis, thyroid gland, adrenal glands and sexual glands).[4] He points out that hatred and fear lead to an increased flow of hormones from the adrenal glands, preparing the body for powerful action. Pleasure, on the other hand, is connected with a slowing down of the nervous system. *Feelings of sexual pleasure cause a regression of brain activity*. This can be demonstrated in the laboratory.

The hypothalamus is not only a sort of relay station, but also contains a group of nerve cells which control the feeling of hunger and the desire for sex and water. Stimulation of the relevant cells prompts a cat to drink much more than it needs. Stimulation of another group of cells makes the cat cease drinking, even though it stands thirsty near the water. The same is true of eating. Also, when a certain group of cells is stimulated, an uncontrollable fit of rage results. Again, the stimulation of still another set of cells causes the cat to lose its anger and its desire to catch. When stimulated, some cells have the power to cause sexual aggression; others cause the animal to lose its sexual interest.

Arousing different nerve centers causes reactions which come quickly and die down just as rapidly. But this is not the case with the sex center. The reaction comes more slowly, stays longer, and is connected with a diminution of brain activity over a period of time.[20]

In human beings the nervous system is designed so that activity above the neck recedes in favor of sexual activity below the diaphragm. "Everyone injured in the spinal cord is a philosopher," said Cushing, the great pioneer of modern neurosurgery. He observed that, in patients with an injury to the spinal cord, which broke the connection between brain and sex organs, *increased brain activity is found in place of sexual activity.* Cushing found that a greater production of ideas, considerations and thoughts existed in such cases.

Research with rats, about which Professor Viktor Frankl reports, is also interesting in this connection.[21] When the rats' sex centers were stimulated with corresponding electrodes, pleasure reactions resulted. The rats were then taught to bring about this pleasure reaction by pressing a button with their paws. Some continually pressed the button; as a result they degenerated sexually to the point of death. In human beings, even in children, *sexual passion can be brought about at will.* If they behave as did the obsessed rats in the above experiment, they too burn themselves out.

It is interesting to note that the above-mentioned evidence contradicts the idea that non-use of sexuality in favor of another work necessarily results in neurosis.

Is Homosexuality Innate or Programmed After Birth?

In seeing more clearly the human possibility for *acquiring* passions, one must regard the position of most homosexual scientists, who maintain that homosexuality is *innate* as self-protective at most. Dr. Schlegel claims he found that male homosexuals have female pelvic measurements.[22] This has not been proven by research on a wide scale. Furthermore, the male homosexual obviously has male hormones and sex organs; why wouldn't he have a male pelvic structure? As far as genetics is concerned, the male homosexual is designed as male, and the lesbian is designed as female.

According to the research of behaviorist Professor Lorenz, the quality of the parent-offspring relationship in animals cannot be known before birth. What can be known is simply the tendency toward such a relationship. Only this tendency is genetically determined. The same is true about the partner relationship. The young animals can be influenced to seek a sexual partner in many ways, including perverse ways: with another of its kind, with a different type of animal, with a human being or even with some inanimate object.

In a very limited way, this suggests that in human beings, too, the tendency toward partnership and procreation is genetically established, but that the sexual quality of the partner, and of the relationship, is determined only after birth. In the case of the homosexual, the determining factors are experiences and encounters of such a nature as to condition the human being in a way opposed to his or her genetic tendency.

The Aggressive Drive and the Sex Drive

Dr. Schlegel maintains that unused sexual energy is converted into aggressive energy, or even into criminality.[22] Other psychologists have similar ideas. Some use as their proof the evidence, during the war, that troops marching into a country which was not sexually encultured experienced a receding of sexual urges and reactions. But these observers forget that other armies moving into areas with sexually extroverted women were not only highly aggressive in battle, but also sexually uninhibited. The downfall of many German tribes, through the influence of the sex-oriented Romans, shows that uninhibited sex activity reduces social energy. The simultaneous loss of the aggressive drive then renders the people incapable of self-defense in times of danger.

In his book *Das sogenannte Boese*, Konrad Lorenz describes the independent functioning of the aggressive drive in its role of defending the existence of the species.[1] Lorenz is of the opinion that the aggressive drive is contained within many other positive human tendencies so that its elimination would have negative results. Naturally, the aggressive drive can join forces with the sex drive, as happens, for example, in rape. But, basically, these drives are independent of each other, and neither is "bad" by nature. The aggressive drive becomes negative only through misuse. Its basic positive goodness is evident in the word "aggressive" itself. The Latin verb *aggredi* includes the positive meaning of approaching another person, as well as the negative aspect of attacking a person or city. The subject's intention makes the aggressive action good or bad.

The constant emergence of evil in the world calls for aggressive response. Precisely today, in the age of pacifism, the absence of the will to fight the powers of degeneration is especially dangerous. Just as an organism absolutely needs the aggressive power to fight off disease, we need a healthy aggressive drive and the right kind of aggressive action. Our lack of "aggression" against the sexual counter-evolution is as deadly a danger as the lack of physical energy to resist and fight infections, disease and cancer.

The human aggressive drive is a specific ability of man to influence and to transform his surrounding. This drive is naturally fed, as are the other drives, by the common energy which the organism has at its disposal. But the moral decision of the individual or of the community determines whether human energy will be used for the preservation of life or for its destruction.

Over-stimulation of the sex drive in heterosexual people produces a condition as difficult to correct as homosexuality. There is no real difference between these conditions regarding the need for subordination to a higher goal within the control of the person. The resulting spiritual tension, if it is sublimated, can lead to corresponding spiritual and cultural accomplishments.

Temporary Receding of the Sex Drive — A Mass Experience

The temporary receding of the sex drive, as a mass experience of soldiers during the war, has already been mentioned. One can assume the following reasons for this experience. The soldiers had a strong motivating goal, even though a wrong one. They were not beset by sexually seducing women — the Russian women around them had only a natural charm, and were much more interested in marriage and family than in sexual escapades. No artificial sexual need was aroused in these men through magazines or films. Their religious connections were stronger than in civilian life. Consequently, their sexual difficulties disappeared almost entirely. As a medical doctor for the troops, I was often asked whether something was put into the soldiers' food to check their sex drive in such a way that it would practically disappear. However, when some men ceased to be motivated by the goal of the war, thinking it criminal or senseless, or when the usual outside stimulations were available, the excessive sex drive of many returned.

When the soldiers finally returned to Germany, it took from four to eight weeks until regular sex urges returned. A similar experience has been reported about men held in prisons and concentration camps. In some cases poor food was partly responsible. Basically, however, the human experience of concentrating all one's energy upon survival was responsible for the receding of the sex drive.

Positive Aggression and Sexual Discipline

What happened to soldiers under negative conditions during the war also can happen when people have positive goals. For example, I had the opportunity of being with a group of 190 young people, as their physician, during a German cultural program in Brazil in 1967. Hardly any other German youth group, with so many handsome young men and women between the ages of fifteen and twenty-five, could have carried out such a program for ten weeks in a foreign country without the occurrence of some sex incidents. However, these particular young people knew beforehand that they could bring about effective relations with Brazilian youth only if they were self-disciplined. Awareness of their responsibility made them capable of the necessary inner discipline, without neuroses or unnatural, warped behavior. Their ability to demonstrate, in our times, the strength of purity and the goodness of clean fun was so unusual that the judgment of all Brazilians whom I met was as follows: "These young people have done more for the reputation of Germany in Brazil, and for young Brazilians, than all groups, taken together, of artists, politicians, and so on, whom you have sent here after the war."

Unlike the mere giving of alms, the right kind of social and cultural help was given in this youth program. The goal was to win Brazilian youth to the fact that they need not waste their creative energies and destroy themselves personally, but that they could express their energy in concrete solutions to their national and international problems. Unless the youth of the developing countries begin to see the need for themselves to become leaders in the development of their land, the problems of those countries will remain unsolved.

In countries other than Brazil, positive results occurred when young people were ready to forgo sexual gratification for the sake of greater goals. Their willingness to work for the right order in human relationships, including the proper relationship of the sexes in the world of tomorrow, became the basis for other social accomplishments.

Here I would like to quote the grandson of Mahatma Gandhi, Rajmohan Gandhi, who wrote in his weekly *Himmat* about the effects on developing countries of Western sex and "pill" propaganda.[23] He said, "Those demanding sex perversion have caused more harm in poor countries during the last twenty years than the imperialists have in the last three hundred years." He disagreed with the view, becoming more and more popular in the West, that selfishness is a virtue, and that adultery, homosexuality and the use of drugs represent a free pass to spiritual experience. He warned, "If Europe causes such ideas to spread abroad, the result in nations like India will be degeneration, poverty and tyranny." In concluding, Rajmohan exclaimed, "What will Europe do in this decade with its unusual dangers and confusion, when hate-filled, revengeful people in Africa, Asia and America already are well along the way on the path of self-destruction! We hope Europe rises. We need a risen Europe which will engage mind and heart in the fight for a better world. . . ."

Biological Indicators of Human Sexual Nature

In an attempt to refute Pope Paul VI on the inseparable connection between sexual union and creation of new life "according to the laws of nature," behaviorist Wickler emphasized parallels between human and animal sexuality (*Stimmen der Zeit,* 1968). He should have begun, instead, with the fundamental biological differences between human and animal sexuality. Actually, he did not even mention the fundamental biological differences which determine corresponding values and societal behavior patterns in all races and nations. He ought to have mentioned the significance of the "hymen," found only in human beings, and the consequent appreciation of virginity, which found its best and most valuable expression in devotion to Mary. The uniqueness of a woman's surrender to a life-long partnership has, here, its biological foundation. Furthermore, Wickler ought to have mentioned the specifically human monthly period of a woman, which constantly reminds her of her fertility and the possibility of new life, just as the disappearance of these periods in menopause reminds her of the cessation of this possibility.

Still further, Wickler should have made a point of the sex diseases that are limited to human beings. Except for premarital sexual intercourse, these diseases would have disappeared from human beings. Precisely from the standpoint of biological nature, venereal sicknesses demand monogamy and premarital chastity. Awareness of the biological danger of sexual license should prompt a sense of responsibility. Knowledge of such facts, unique to human beings, ought to result in a wholesome formation of conscience.

A sense of shame, too, is characteristic of human beings. In no way is shame an artificial or unnatural "taboo." It is a result of the vulnerability of virginity and of the personal wholeness of the human being. When these are penetrated by an unauthorized third person, the innermost sphere of love and union between two people is destroyed. Destruction of these qualities has no positive advantage; the result is that persons become "things." Whoever makes a "thing" of a human being destroys the person and brutalizes him. Freud is supposed to have said, "The loss of shame is the beginning of feeblemindedness."

A Sense of Shame versus Pornography

Even some higher animals have a sense of shame and definite "taboos" in the realm of sexuality. When a dolphin is born, the mother withdraws into shallow water and other female dolphins form a circle around her. No male is permitted to enter until the mother dolphin is ready to present her young. Today, for financial profit we show human births on television. This is the same prostitution of human intimacy as having sexual relations for money.

If one may, or even "must," show in pictures everything which is "natural," because one wishes to be "honest," is there any limit to pornography? Even some theologians think not. This is why a Bavarian chaplain deliberately took his secondary school students to sex films in order to be able to discuss them "scientifically" afterwards. Other theologians promote parents' swimming in the nude with their children. They maintain that the biblical story of Adam and Eve, so essential for man and his development, is now out-dated. The scriptural passage, "they realized that they were naked and were ashamed and hid themselves; they sewed fig leaves together and made loin cloths for themselves," is ridiculed as meaningless. Such people understand little or nothing of the essence of human sexuality.

The new breed of theologians not only misunderstand the

religious-cultural implications of pornography but also its psychological impact. They fail to realize that the subconscious mind is damaged even more than the conscious mind, and that the total human person is affected. Explicit pictures have the power to influence our actions and character positively or negatively. As long as we are able to balance the negative impressions with a corresponding number of positive impressions, our freedom and self-control generally are maintained.

If, however, it is impossible to maintain this balance, if negative impressions supersede the positive, the person is negatively conditioned. By viewing the intimate sexual union of two persons, the intrusive third person perverts that union into exhibitionism, prostitution and harlotry, even if the watcher is a camera. This negative impression cannot be balanced by a positive impression in the subconscious mind as long as the positive impression is another picture of sexual intercourse, since the picture changes the act to a negative impression. Exhibited sex or sold sexuality always reduces persons to the level of *things*, always exploits them for selfish reasons.

Exhibited sex, therefore, is pornography. The viewing of such pictures make the male viewer incapable of seeing his wife as anything but a prostitute. The female is similarly affected regarding her husband.

When people like Dr. Siegusch, Professor Mitscherlich, Mr. Kentler and others maintain that "pornography is not socially harmful," that its bad effects have not been "scientifically" proven, that their efforts have shown the contrary, namely, that there are no negative effects of pornography, one must wonder what profits they stand to gain. Are they making money as psychological counsellors for the advertising business, an obvious area of sexual exploitation for gain?

One cannot expect those with ulterior motives to be honest about the effects of pornography. Naturally, one cannot expect a psychology professor (divorced from his wife of the first marriage with two children, divorced from his wife of the second marriage with three children, and whose third wife promotes abortion) to admit publicly that family breakups, and the consequent psychological effect on the children, are socially harmful.

By doing so he would openly condemn himself. Likewise, one can hardly expect that the supporters of homosexuality would oppose pornography, the necessary propaganda instrument for changing public consciousness and normal human feelings about homosexuality. Only when every perversion and display of lust has the same public rights as normal human behavior, can these people expect acceptance for their own selfish perversion. In such a social environment it can easily happen that a man like Mr. Verch, instructor in "the science of sex" on the faculty at Hamburg, would say in his highly recommended second-rate book that pornography is harmless for children and that it is for them a "help to masturbation." [7]

Why Must Pornography Be Forbidden?

Because the pattern of behavior it depicts is pure sex without love, pornography has a destructive effect on many relationships. Indeed, it shows the purely selfish pleasure of manipulating others and the sadistic destruction and debasement of the partner. After giving a television talk against pornography, one medical doctor received 120 telephone calls from women who wanted to tell him that their marriage had been ruined by pornography. The following letter is typical of the catastrophic harm pornography has on couples, married as well as unmarried:

> I have never before bought an illustrated newspaper. However, the headline 'We are no automatons as far as love is concerned' struck me at once and I bought the newspaper. I can only say that you are justified in your complaints. Unfortunately we are all too cowardly to fight this 'wave of nudity' and are happy when someone else has the courage to do so publicly.
>
> There is, God knows, nothing of sex left to imagine. In spite of this, people run to every sex film that is being shown.
>
> Formerly I had no complaints about my husband's conduct, but since the appearance of the sex films, he has changed. Now he is merely a "bull performing to capacity," if you will, please, excuse the expression. And because I can no longer respond to him with what he desires, he calls me a frigid, uninterested old grandmother. I know there are many people who are not interested in daily sexual intercourse. I have often nearly despaired

about my husband's lack of concern. He scarcely waits for the end of my period. I can be sick or not in form, but that makes no difference to him. This was not the case formerly. I know with certitude that this change was caused in him by sex films because we were happily married for ten years before the films arrived.

I hate to see him go to a sex film, for when he returns he falls upon me like a wild animal and I offer him too little. He even demands presentations a la striptease. I could write a novel about it. I only hope things will change some day, although that is difficult to imagine now.

I write this because it proves you are right. Forgive my anonymity, but you will understand that I do not wish to expose my husband and myself.

I thank you for your courage, for I can imagine that you have made enemies because of your stand.

At another time, a woman doctor wrote to me:

I am a doctor by profession. Thus I am definitely not a prude, unaccustomed to the sight of nude bodies. However, when I view a nude body, often in a very suggestive pose, on the magazine rack I feel insulted and have the feeling of standing there myself — even though I am no longer as young and beautiful as these ladies are — exposed to the gaze of all who pass by. By nature a human being possesses a sense of shame, even if today efforts are being made to deny this. This sense of shame is very advanced even among primitive peoples. Recently I spoke to a lady who lived in Africa for years. She related that Negroes, accustomed to wearing sparse clothing, were horrified when they saw an illustrated magazine from the West. They regarded these picture magazines as shameless and refused them altogether.

Since pornography violates the human capacity for love and marriage, openly degrading the dignity of the human person and the human procreative act, it is a spiritual and psychological disease. As such, it should be resisted by a nation, just as other contagious diseases and infections are resisted. Personal pollution should be corrected by the state just as physical pollution is corrected. The pornographic disease can destroy a nation's cultural credibility, injure the bonds of international laws and agreements, and devastate ideological and political understanding. It destroys freedom.[24] But most of all, it erodes the most intimate realm of marriage and family. For these serious reasons, the societal taboo against pornography must be upheld.

Whoever wants to contract a contagious spiritual disease, thus making himself incapable of love and the miracle of genuine marriage and family, is naturally free to do so. But that person is just as foolish and infantile as one who deliberately exposes himself to the pox.

We have been hearing that since pornography has been freely permitted in Denmark, sexual crimes have been reduced in that country. This represents a willful distortion of the facts! Naturally, if the presentation and picturing of all types of sex perversion are permitted, the number of reported sexual crimes must decrease. Who would then feel obliged to report any such crime? Furthermore, if the sex violator is regarded by psychologists and judges as a victim of circumstances, who would assume the inconvenience of a useless court case? The victim of the crime is then regarded as the unlucky person, similar to one who has the misfortune of being in a car accident. The truth about Denmark's situation is that, in 1973 alone, after the free use of pornography was promoted, the number of rapes and indecent assaults in Baden-Wuerttemberg increased by eighteen percent.

The Reaction of Developing Countries to Imported "Sexual Freedom"

The anti-baby "pill" and sexual freedom propaganda exported by Western white countries to countless developing countries have negatively affected family structures in these countries. The result has been a growing reaction against the "degenerated white exploiters." And the criticism is deserved.

It was the whites who created the conditions for an explosive increase in population in the first place. Through their patronizing sanitation and medical improvement, as well as through their industrial development and exploitation of colored peoples, the whites helped reduce the death rate, increase the birth rate, and increase life expectancy in the developing countries. But they failed to combine technological growth with moral values and clear social goals.

Instead, the whites brought along their pornographic films, newspapers, magazines, and the corresponding conduct of their visitors and tourists. The same impression of moral corruption is given to students, athletes, workers and diplomats from developing countries who visit Europe and the United States. Reactions of contempt for us are increasing.

At the world cultural conference of UNESCO in 1970, under the leadership of the Soviet Minister of Culture, Furtsewa, a vehement discussion about this corruptive white influence took place between the "non-Christian" peoples of Islam, Hinduism, Buddhism, communism, and the "formerly Christian" nations of the West. Western nations were accused of destroying the cultural structures of developing nations by the export of their "pleasure industry." The "non-Christians" demanded that this export be stopped. In spite of the objection of West Germans, Scandinavians and Americans, a majority vote against pornography was reached. This vote put a binding duty on all member countries of UNESCO "to guarantee the observance of commonly recognized moral and educational principles in public films, television and radio programs." [24]

And the result in Germany? All those who otherwise wanted renewed relationships with the Eastern countries fought passionately for the "rights" of pornography. Indeed, they began to demand an official withdrawal from those international agreements and pacts according to which Germany, along with other nations, was bound to fight against pornography for fifty years. All for the sake of some sexual psychopaths and a few sex capitalists!

One must wonder whether politicians who so easily permit the destruction of the human environment and of their own nation's credibility are not themselves sexual psychopaths. Or, perhaps they wish to give communism active help. In fact, the free use of pornography was one of the most important ideological victories of communism over the Federal Republic of Germany. Even Minister President Kohl (CDU) was ultimately guilty of the political compromise which permitted this to happen.

Finally, it is clear that combining the export of sexual degeneration along with aid for mass sterilization and mass abortion results in still more extreme mistrust of the West in developing countries. They sense that this double exportation inevitably must destroy the national structures and cultures of their lands.

The Statement of the Medical Doctors of Ulm Is Verified

As early as 1964, in a statement made by the medical doctors of Ulm, the bad consequences that would follow from our policies in the developing countries were alluded to. This warning appears in Part III, sections 3 and 4 of the statement. "A help in development which leads only to sanitary, medical and material progress but not to the development of people to act responsibly and to reach a democratic order resting upon self-government necessarily creates more problems than it solves and will act like a real boomerang for us.

"It is, therefore, not our task for purely business reasons to force methods which are contrary to their best traditions and standards upon black nations for the solution of their population problems. If we do so, we put ourselves in danger of looking down upon colored people as if they are incapable of developing themselves into clean, responsible personalities." [19]

The grandson of Mahatma Gandhi, Rajmohan Gandhi, sharing the opinion of his grandfather, addressed himself to this question in his weekly *Himmat*: "Among the solutions which are suggested for overcoming need in countries like ours, the forced introduction of birth control through contraceptives and sterilization represents one of the most naïve and dangerous apparent solutions. . . ."

One of his co-workers spoke as follows at a world conference held in Europe: "These so-called educated people oppose discipline in their own lives. Thus they do not believe that the power of God can purify people. . . . Why can they not regard us as mature, intelligent people and expect the most of us . . . ?" [25]

Professor Dr. Hans Luxenburger, Munich psychiatrist and former co-worker of Siegmund Freud, wrote in a letter footnoting his signature to the statement of the medical doctors of Ulm, "The term 'anti-baby pill' alone says volumes. One can call a pill which hinders the appearance of maw-worms the 'anti-maw-worm pill.' Analogously the 'anti-baby pill' is a pill which protects against the appearance of babies. The child, apparently, is put on a level with intestinal parasites — a standpoint which betrays a remarkable level of ethical consciousness in him who discovered the name, and in those who, agreeing with that meaning, use such 'pills.' One can only say that they do not give it a thought because thinking is generally not their strength, and often thinking human beings use the word without even putting it into quotation marks."

In some countries, therefore, "anti-baby pills" are the "hated, white imported pills," which are supposed to prevent the existence of more colored people, just like remedies used against parasites. Similarly, the United States Supreme Court ruling permitting abortion upon request up to the end of the sixth month is interpreted by colored people as a measure against the "flood" of black births. This is the way the situation looks today to many black leaders. Someday, when the countless physical deformities which are expected to follow prolonged use of the "pill " become noticeable, this "pill" import will become an even more bitter source of hatred toward the degenerated white man.

Naturally, Rajmohan Gandhi, like many other responsible politicians in developing countries, knows that the old sex morality is no longer adequate for the new sociological situation. The marriages of children, need for housing, social misery, and definite religious customs in India; the ideas of power and social position connected with large families in Africa; the strong sense of family among the Chinese; promiscuity in the slums of South America; and many other conditions and customs present problems that do not seem to have a single solution in terms of proper sexual behavior. But it is certain that the danger of overpopulation in the developing nations cannot be adequately met by means of sterilization, abortion and "anti-baby pills," even if some intellectuals think otherwise. Bertrand Russell went so far as to demand free access to all these methods, and the use of police power to force resisting churches to conform, regardless of their moral principles.

According to authoritative specialists, the problem of world hunger could be avoided without the use of sterilization, mass abortions and "anti-baby pills." This could happen if nations would promote birth control through the control of sex; if they would promote better methods of farming, and if they would open new farming areas and improve ways of using available water and food. According to these specialists, it would be entirely possible to feed many of the world's people. One example is the Dutch doctor Karl Gunning, of Rotterdam, who worked for a long time in developing countries. In his book *Psychologie der Menschheit*, he shows that there are ways of handling population problems other than by the hysterical cry for "anti-baby pills," and the resulting destruction of sexual morality.[26]

Naturally, every educational process takes time! However, the decisive prerequisite for overcoming massive problems through education is a valid ideal that serves as a type of "genetic information" for humanity. This universal idea is an answer to the question as to why, and for what purpose, a new order must come about. Such an ideal must be based on valid ideas of good and evil for all human relationships. A structureless moral chaos can be overcome only by means of clear standards and a readiness to accept them everywhere. These standards should be valid for all areas of life, private and public. If clear standards are not established for the most intimate of human relationships — if the way to unity, purity, truth and peace is not found in this area of life — it will remain forever an illusion in life's larger areas, which are more difficult to interpret and govern.

Overcoming a Relative, Old Morality through Absolute Moral Standards

How can one think about establishing common standards among peoples with various customs and morals? Is this not an impossible Utopia?

But besides having different customs, ideas and laws, the various cultures have different systems of weight, measurement, numerical and alphabetic symbols. In spite of these differences, common measurement, alphabet and number systems, which are understood everywhere in the world, have been developed. Those who refused to accept these common standards and who wanted to retain their old, relative, indefinite standards simply excluded themselves from the general scientific and technological development of mankind.

The metric system has been widely accepted. Systems for measuring temperature or electricity (volts, amperes, watts), and the Arabic number system have been standardized. By means of electronics, absolute standards of technology can be realized universally.

The complexity of our increasingly technical civilization forces an even more precise measurement of reality in order to prevent terrible disasters. For example, a trip to the moon with the weights and measures of the Middle Ages would be unthinkable. Instead of eliminating out-dated and useless standards, technology has refined them to the point of an absolute standard.

Analogously, the same principle of refinement is involved in the development of society as a whole. It is clear that out-dated laws and standards hinder development. But lawlessness creates chaos and destroys everything. For that reason, the answer to the failure of the old morality, and the recent discovery of cultural relativity in the area of morals, cannot be a mere situation ethics or each person deciding what is right and wrong in his own situation. Today, so many claim to be following their "consciences." But conscience, if it is to be properly functional, needs "certain knowledge" about commonly valid and binding behavioral norms.

If nations, classes and races are to be united in a world community, different ideas of morality must be brought together under a common idea of right and wrong; they must be refined to the point of absolute moral standards, acceptable to, and binding upon, everyone.

In all ages, universal human rights and freedom have been proclaimed. The world wars have intensified these proclamations. However, as long as we do not move beyond the proclamation of rights and freedom to affirmative practice of absolute moral standards, such proclamations are hollow moralisms which are politically misused in order to remind the next person, or the next nation, of faults against his own freedom and rights. "Everyone hopes the next person will change, and every nation desires improvement in others, but no one wants to begin by changing himself." [27] That is the main problem. Moral standards are not a catalogue of personal rights and freedoms but, before all else, standards for one's own responsibility, decision and actions.

Just as various people can develop themselves only by adopting universal standards in technology, personal and national moral progress can be made only to the extent that absolute moral standards are understood and subjectively lived by all together.

Points of Orientation for Spiritual-Moral Standards of Life

Regarding the need for universally accepted moral standards, the first questions are: where do these standards come from, and how can we establish and enforce them?

Forces determining our standards and laws must be the protection and development of human beings, the meaning and goal of life, and the need for a functioning society. We have two main possibilities for orientation:

a) scientific knowledge,
b) religious "revealed" knowledge.

From the standpoint of scientific knowledge, five points of orientation present themselves for the derivation of moral standards:

1. the historical
2. the political
3. the biological
4. the psychological
5. the sociological

The History of Man, in the Development of His Freedom and Rationality, as a Point of Orientation for Moral Standards

Since this question has been thoroughly treated by professionals like the behaviorist Konrad Lorenz, I would like simply to summarize their views and to point out a few important features. As was mentioned in the first part of this book, Lorenz revealed that animal instincts are genetically anchored behavioral norms which are necessary for the preservation and development of the species. He points out especially "four great" drives: the hunger drive, the sex drive, the aggressive drive and the escape drive.

He is convinced that, in man, these four drives are in no way bad urges, but rather impulses which foster life, and without which we cannot exist. As long as the hunger drive serves the preservation and higher development of life, it is good. But when it converts into passion, greed, and an instrument for the suppression and exploitation of others, it becomes a destroyer of life. The same is true about the sex drive. Whenever sex is creative in terms of community formation, it is good. But when it is used for the exploitation of others and simply for the purposes of erotic pleasure, it destroys individual and community life.

Also, the aggressive drive, when it acts to protect life and community, is good. The aggression of hate, which knows only its own egoism, destroys life and therefore is bad. The use of aggression for the accomplishment of great purposes is necessary for the existence of human culture and is the basis of true love.

The drive to escape, based on genuine knowledge that we are not Titans or gods, and that we must not take senseless risks, is necessary to life. Genuine humility is never cowardice. However, arrogance and pride, based on a false evaluation of one's own strength, leads to the destruction of oneself and others.

From these simple truths, clear behavioral norms for individuals and communities originate spontaneously. Lorenz thinks that life-preserving instincts and morals in man, if they are right, are similar to those in animals. He is also of the opinion that moral laws are the natural laws of human life in community. In connection with his explanation of various theories of human freedom, he wrote in the previously mentioned book, *Das sogenannte Boese*, as follows:

> Only to the superficial eye does freedom of will seem to be doing as one wills in complete disregard of law. . . . No one can seriously believe that free will implies permitting the caprice of an individual, like that of an irresponsible tyrant, to decide what ought or ought not to be done. Our free will is subject to the strict laws of morality, and our desire for freedom is present to hinder us from obeying laws other than moral laws. Signifi-

cantly, the fearful feeling of lack of freedom is never produced by the knowledge that our actions are bound to the laws of physics. We all know that the greatest and finest freedom of human beings is identical with the moral law within them.

Human development toward higher freedom and meaning in life, as studied in the first part of this book, is unthinkable without absolute behavioral norms. The correct evolutionary effort of human drives, therefore, presupposes the development of a responsible personality capable of self-control and free decisions.

For example, the formation of a family presupposes the integration of the sex drive into the controls of personality. The fact that a human being needs about eighteen years until he is capable of handling existence alone implies that his parents must be mutually responsible for him during that time. Because of parents' mutual responsibility toward children, life-long monogamy becomes a human norm. There is no reason why a wife should be condemned to a harem, without having as much security as a grey goose, which lives in a monogamous partnership.

Conduct directed by evolutionary standards disposes the four drives for the balanced fulfillment of life. The perversion of these drives, on the other hand, militates against the human ability to respond to norms for an evolutionary purpose.

The Political Point of Orientation

It has already been shown that human beings can exist in peace as a world community only when individuals and groups conduct themselves according to common binding moral standards. In his well-known talk on peace, Professor Carl Friedrich von Weizaecker said that "world peace can be maintained only through an unusual moral effort." [28] Consonant with this point, Professor Dr. Georg Picht of Heidelberg said at the end of his book *Mut zur Utopie*:

> In the current phase of our civilization it appears that the material and physical existence of humanity depends exclusively on the spiritual and moral powers of human nature. Political and scientific reason disposes of the fate of mankind. [Professor Picht understands "reason" not as pure *ratio* or intellect but as respon-

sible thinking and acting before mankind's future, and also ultimately before God.] However, since our political order and our
sciences have disintegrated and are, therefore, no longer reasonable, the future of mankind depends on whether or not we can
succeed in establishing a new level of collective morality in a
qualitative transition, thus reaching a new level of collective reason. Mankind will be able to master the future only through a
moral and spiritual breakthrough for which no example exists in
history until now.[29]

However, this "new level of collective morality" is the same
need as that which we have for common, absolute, moral standards. The laws which hold for the microcosm are prerequisites for
the laws which are valid for the macrocosm; they do not lose their
validity in the larger, more complex organism. Physical laws are
prerequisites for chemical laws. Physical and chemical principles
are prerequisites for biological laws. Thus, it is unthinkable that
one could establish world peace without standards which have
validity for all areas of human life.

At all levels of society, the prerequisites for peace are trust and
cooperation. On the other hand, lies and deceit, exploitation and
hatred, rape, murder, terror, war and bloody revolution destroy
a marriage just as much as they do a world community. Trust
exists only on the basis of absolute honesty and the renunciation
of every type of exploitation, whether in business, politics or sex.
Honest and just motives are prerequisites for every type of peace,
including world peace.

"Love of mankind" is an empty ideal if love is not practiced
in the smallest unit of society, the family. The "qualitative transition to a new level of collective morality" and the "spiritual and
moral breakthrough for which there has been no example in
history until now" [29] must be made by each individual person, and
practiced in small societal units if it is to succeed in larger units.

The Biological Point of Orientation

We have already observed the fact that our own organism
can exist only because its elementary parts — atoms, molecules,
cells and organs — respond to each other according to definite,

codified, physical, chemical and biological standards, and because these parts integrate themselves into the higher quality and order of a superior whole. The price for this higher existence is always a partial surrender of "individualistic" independence. Integration of parts within a whole belongs to the reality of every higher form of being. And this higher totality, because of its higher plan, its more complex structure, its new order, quality and function — in other words, because of its higher "being" — is more than the mere sum of its parts.

Just as living parts of an organism have the power to integrate themselves, they also have the possibility of again "freeing themselves" from the order in which they exist. In other words, they can break away and revolt. In the realm of living organisms, we call the degeneration of a higher form of being "death." A revolt by individual parts against the higher quality of the whole produces the death of that whole. In reference to our bodies we call the beginning of the revolt against the whole "sickness." When organs revolt we speak of "sick organs." The stomach, heart, kidneys, etc., "revolt," giving us "stomach disorders," etc. The cells which do not want to accommodate themselves to a higher structure, such as a bacillus, cancer cell or an anti-cell, can destroy the body. The protein molecule which does not integrate itself into the structure of the organism can destroy the whole entity. The atoms and quanta which *autonomously* produce electronic signals in our nervous system revolt against our person and cause mental illness.

Also, when our drives, emotions and will are not directed according to correct societal laws, neuroses result. Neuroses are produced, too, when society makes it impossible for the individual to reach meaning in life. Through the individual's revolt, an atomizing of human groups results. We call these revolts crime, sin, guilt. Naturally every revolt of parts against the higher whole has concrete reasons.

This fundamental principle (parts in relation to a whole) functions on all levels of existence. Even in the lowest levels of the inorganic world there is a sort of freedom of individual parts. Uranium and radium atoms demonstrate this freedom and spontaneity. In his book *Modernizing Man*, Dr. Campbell quotes from the physicist Professor Pasqual Jordan's book *Wissenschaft und Geschichte* as follows:

> When we observe individual atoms which build up gigantic bodies and quantities of things, we find free, individual decisions not determined by the natural law, everywhere.
>
> Thus organic life participates in the same freedom and spontaneity which the physicists found at the root of material being. . . . In other words, the attempt to prove that man is a machine and has no free will has been factually disproved by science.[30]

A Relevant Analogy

The degeneration of higher organisms, through the revolt of a part against superior structures, is especially evident in cancer. Every cell — with the exception of the red blood corpuscle — has within its nucleus the structural plan of the whole organism. Because the cell possesses the guiding ideal of the larger whole, it has the ability to constantly orientate itself toward the goals of the whole. It also has the ability to reproduce, to renew itself, and to eliminate poisons, viruses and waste products which do not promote the well-being of the whole structure. Speaking analogously, there is "knowledge within the cell" about "evil" and "good."

According to contemporary opinions, cancer begins with a "mutation" in the nucleus of a cell. This destruction of the guiding ideal within its genetic center of information robs the cell of its superior orientation and leads it to bad behavior. We recognize cancer in the freedom of the cell to indiscriminately multiply itself. It no longer serves healthy growth and renewal; rather, it serves its own egotism and its own revolt against the entire organism.

Cancer is recognizable in the primitive form of its own cell. While the healthy cell has a form corresponding to its special function, the cancer cell takes on the form of the amoeba, becoming round or spindle-shaped and having only a loose connection with neighboring cells. Because its guiding ideal has been destroyed in its nucleus, cancer is not able to form its own structure. The cancerous growth degenerates within and grows at the edges of healthy tissues, on which it feeds. Only hard connective tissue, and an intolerant limiting and starving out of the cancer, can halt it. Constant "dialogue" and exchange of material, which causes cancer to poison healthy cells and weaken the whole organism, cannot halt cancerous growth.

Similarly, the degeneration of a culture begins with the destruction of its guiding ideal and its behavioral norms. Without the guiding image, the conscience in the nucleus of the individual no longer functions correctly. The consequent disintegration of the social organism cannot be halted unless there remains some hard connective social tissue and social intolerance to the spreading disease. In order to cure a person suffering from cancer, the body's power to resist cancerous growth must be restored. This is done by removing all poison from the metabolism of normal cells and from the entire organism. Detoxification, along with good nutrition, is necessary.

The liberalistic tendency to remove penal laws against perverted behavior is similar to eliminating the power to resist cancer and creating a defenseless co-existence with cancer cells. But we already know that "pluralistic" co-existence with egotistical cancer cells causes the death of the entire organism.

Therefore, the answer to the sexual revolt in contemporary society is not "dialogue" with the "sex revolutionaries," but the inner renewal and purification of human individuals who are still responsible to some degree. Constant inner detoxification of individual minds and emotions is necessary for the good health of the social organism.

The Psychological Point of Orientation

The relation of the four drives to the "will to meaning," discussed earlier in this book, is another source of moral orientation. The reversed meanings of these drives — sexual passion, gluttony, drunkenness, greed, etc., can be *causes* for loss of meaning in life, as well as *results* of a life empty of meaning. As was already pointed out, a suppressed "will to meaning" can cause neurotic illness. Such a suppression and resultant neurosis can be the effect of one's own disoriented will or behavior. It can also be the effect of societal exploitation of the individual. Persons can be forced to sacrifice the authentic goal of life to false ideological goals of the society.

Besides the tension between individual and society, life's many other tensions can become sources of neurosis. There are tensions between wanting to act and being unable to act, between satisfaction of desires and satisfaction of conscience, between self and other. Such tensions can be transferred to our bodies and cause organic neurosis. They can be transferred to our spiritual-mental life and cause psychoneurosis.

The neurotic resolution of tension usually involves a dishonest settlement of discord. By adapting oneself to false societal pressures because of fear of eventual disadvantage, one resorts to self-deceit. This is done by rationalizing one's capitulation to anti-human and anti-divine goals as "tolerance" or "love of peace." At the same time, one is forced to camouflage one's own egotistical motives in order to preserve some self-respect. And one must blame circumstances and other people for the whole situation.

It is a common human tendency of self-preservation to camouflage a crisis organically, mentally or spiritually. But if this camouflage becomes an automatic habit or a permanent reflex, it becomes a serious lie to oneself and to others. This profound deceit then rules one's life and forms the kernel of his organic or psychological neurosis. The cure for such neurosis is radical honesty.

In the case of a neurosis originating in a rationalized capitulation to societal selfishness, radical honesty means courage to obey God rather than man. It means a decision to hold on to the divine meaning in life and to affirm absolute behavioral norms. The great lie dissolves and eventually the neurosis disappears.

Under certain circumstances, such radical honesty can mean that one is prepared to risk money, property, position, health, freedom and life, as Solzhenitsyn and his friends have done. That is the way to freedom taken by all those men and women, in the past and present, who have been prepared to become martyrs for their convictions, and who have fought for inner conversion of the society until its order corresponded with the real meaning of human life.

In the case of a neurosis originating in a conflict between personal selfishness and true societal norms, radical honesty means affirmation of these words: "The truth will make you free!" Readiness to admit one's motives, goals, actions, and also one's dishonesty is the only remedy. The cure of such a neurosis, therefore, does not come from an unchecked expression of inner drives, but, as mentioned earlier, through meaning-therapy or logotherapy.[21] This form of treatment places the creative powers and the "tension potential" of the neurotic in the context of a meaningful relationship and gives his "will to meaning" a chance to integrate his drives. The person then is able to realize himself in honesty. This standard of honesty is necessary for psycho-physical health in both the individual and the community.

Ideology-Neurosis

Since modern ideologies of liberalism, nationalism, communism, humanism and pacifism elevate a partial value to the status of an absolute value, these ideologies distort human reality.

When the individual's private lie becomes society's public lie, a mass neurosis or mass psychosis results. There is no cure other than absolute honesty. In his famous "open letter" to the Soviet leaders, Aleksandr I. Solzhenitsyn shows us the only way to cure such mass psychosis.[31] In the appendix of his letter he says: "Do not live with lies!" And he shows that false systems can lose their power only if hundreds and thousands of people resist. They must be determined to speak, to write and to tolerate only what is true. A lie dies when truth is strong. And a lying system becomes powerless when its lie loses its hold. "This," says Solzhenitsyn, "is not an easy way, but it is the easiest of all possible ways." This is not an easy choice for the body, but "the only one for the soul," and it leads to freedom and to the cure of ideology-neurosis.

A False Cure for Neurosis

Tension is necessary for all living things. An attempt to get rid of tension, including healthy tension, is a false way of treating neurosis. Tensions, which discharge without control, act like lightning that causes fire, injuries and death. Just because of the dangers of electrical high voltage, we do not decide to get rid of all electrical power. Instead, we attempt to build greater security and to direct valuable power into constructive uses.

Life is sustained and developed by an uninterrupted effort to balance tension and entropy (tension loss). This is done by constantly building up new tensions. If the process fails, the result is death.

What is true of atomic power is also true of tension. *The greater the energy potential, the greater the positive possibilities in a controlled discharge, as well as the negative destruction in an uncontrolled, senseless or wrong discharge.*

One of man's strongest tension potentials is manifested in the sex drive. This tension potential is maintained in every genuine culture by the development of a sense of shame through clothing, customs, etc. Present-day efforts to eliminate a sense of shame are also a way of eliminating erotic tension. However, the organism quickly attempts to build up tension again. And when this tension is constantly discharged in an uncontrolled manner, a compulsive passion is formed. This is an unbalanced and neurotic condition that often ends in meaninglessness. Loss of meaning, in turn, reinforces a rampant growth of isolated sex.

Professor Buerger Prinz, well-known psychiatrist from Hamburg, said in a Hamburg paper that already there are more cases of neurosis resulting from excessive sexual freedom than all cases taken together that resulted from sexual prudery. The psychoanalytic attempt to cure neurosis by reducing a genuine awareness of guilt, and by uncontrolled expression of suppressed drives, *is not really successful.* The uncontrolled expression of one's drives, at the expense of meaningful moral norms, causes neurotic tensions of fear, hatred and greed, and leads to a multiplication of neuroses.

"Modern" psychotherapists try to cure stomach cramps and heart-palpitation by reducing the individual's norms of life and the guilt feelings caused by these norms. Such a method ultimately leads to wrong meaning or complete loss of meaning in life. As a result, people with whom the person lives tend to become neurotic also. If we imagine a society where every member expresses an uncontrolled need for sexual pleasure in order to avoid neurosis, we would have to imagine a battle of all against all. In reality there is enough to satisfy everyone's need, but there is not enough to satisfy everyone's greed.

It would be worth a thorough examination to discover the effects of a "cured" neurotic on his family and surroundings. The case of a pastor comes to mind. The *psychoanalytic* cure of his "cardiac neurosis" led to gall bladder attacks in his wife, to neurotic disturbances in his children, and ended in divorce. An authentic cure would not have affected the man's family in such a destructive way. Even if neurotic tension does disappear in an individual case, the therapeutic method that subordinates moral norms to raw drives is socially harmful. Harmony between unconscious urges and conscious action is wrongly achieved by adjusting the conscious mind to suit unconscious wishes. Harmony can be achieved authentically by a complete reorientation of motives and drives to a higher meaning in life. Inner tensions and neurosis can be resolved when conscious desires and unconscious urges serve the same meaning and goal. This happens through a change of heart, a new awareness of responsibility toward others, and a readiness to be completely honest in the recognition of motives and true guilt. Without a balanced sense of guilt, the constant regeneration of motives needed for human development would not be possible.

The Cross as the Answer to Neurosis

According to our present-day consumer society, the ideal human being is one who is free from suffering and tensions, without aggression, constantly enjoying "happiness," dull, bored, pleasure-loving and success-minded. He is capable neither of love nor hatred. He is incapable of the creative accomplishments necessary to solve the problems of mankind today. On the contrary, the person who is "of age" will be one who directs tension into positive effort, not one who exists merely by reducing his tensions.

Christ was neither a neurotic nor an aggressor. He endured

tensions resulting from the conflict between human self-will, his human drives, and the will of God. But the highest will to meaning, God's will, overcame all these tensions so that, completely conscious and aware, He accepted a criminal death on the Cross. *The Cross itself has since become the symbol of the transformation of the greatest tension by the noblest surrender and highest accomplishment. It is the sign of the transformation of the most extreme aggression of hatred by a radical expression of love.* In the history of the last two thousand years, nothing has contributed so much to the spiritual change, inner renewal and higher meaning of mankind. The Cross has changed the entire world.

This surrender of the greatest human tensions, impulses and energies to the highest meaning in God's plan, a surrender for which the Cross stands, has since become the only real alternative of hope in the face of threats of world annihilation, mass sex neurosis and other human meaninglessness. In answer to the danger of sexual neurosis, Christ saw no reason to diminish norms of purity and self-discipline. He demanded, instead, the control of one's sex drive.

A modern version of the text, "If your eye is your downfall, gouge it out. . . . If your hand or foot is your undoing, cut it off . . ." (Matthew 16:8) might well read, "Prefer to make allowances for the physical harm of neurosis rather than permit the revolt of your sex drive." Christian faith is not just a sentimental feeling which permits one to do as he pleases because he is regarded as being incapable of discipline. This faith does not advocate a relaxation of one's drives at the expense of others.

It does invite a meaningful endurance of the greatest tension and a transformation of desires, emotions, thoughts and energy into a creative, God-controlled existence. This transformation is our only chance to overcome misguided meanings as well as passions of hatred, avarice, lust, greed, fear and hunger for power. The greatest men and women in history have experienced the change from negative aggressive motives to constructive love. St. Francis of Assisi, Mahatma Gandhi, Buddha, St. Paul, Nicholas of Fluee, Frank Buchman, Werenfried von Straaten, Bodelschwingh, Mother Cabrini and Peter Howard are among them.

On the other hand, individuals who use their energy potential solely for their own pleasure and satisfaction are incapable of love's great accomplishments.

The necessary change from negative aggression and selfish satisfaction of desires to positive, responsible accomplishments of love demands the redeeming inspiration of a power outside the human personality. William Penn put it this way: "Human beings must decide to let God rule them or they will damn themselves to being ruled by tyrants."

When Willy Brandt, then mayor of Berlin, telephoned Dr. Frank Buchman in the United States to congratulate him on his last birthday, Buchman quoted William Penn's statement to Brandt. It was the tragedy of Willy Brandt, as it was of so many others in Western politics, that he was not ready to make that decision. He believed he could cover up his past with good will, and carry out successful peace politics without accepting absolute behavioral norms of honesty. Similar was the tragedy of Richard Nixon, who got involved in the Watergate scandal by being unwilling to betray his friends. He failed to recognize that mutual trust and, therefore, absolute honesty are necessary for successful politics in the free world.

The Sociological Point of Orientation
Sexual Discipline and the Rise of Social Creativity

In examining the rise and fall of human cultures, the sociologists I. D. Unwin, author of *Sex and Culture*,[32] and Pitirim Sorokin, author of *The American Sex Revolution*, arrived at the conclusion that a close relationship exists between discipline in sexual behavior and the rise of social creativity.[33] Without "the sacrifice of drives" it would be impossible to develop what we call culture and civilization. Unwin offers a number of proofs for the connection between sexual discipline, or the lack of it, and the respective rise or decline of culture in the areas of politics, economics, culture and religion. Examining all high cultures and the eighty primitive cultures still existing today, he proves that, without exception, there is a correlation between the degree of premarital abstinence from sex and the degree of religious and political development in a culture.

All societies with a cultivated faith in God, evidenced by the presence of priests and temples, were developed during a period in which premarital chastity was demanded by law — at least for women. On the other hand, societies with strong ancestor and spirit worship were not as firmly demanding of premarital chastity. Finally, those societies which had neither temples nor faith nor belief in life after death allowed total freedom in premarital sex. For that reason, Unwin concludes that the limiting of sexual freedom is necessary for the development and free use of human "social energy" in spiritual, political and economic accomplishments. "One cannot long enjoy the advantages of a high level of spiritual culture while permitting sexual license at the same time. To do so contradicts the endurance and strength of human nature." [32]

A modern example of this cultural principle can be found in Red China. The Red Chinese have disdained the public sexuality of white imperialists. Mao Tse Tung radically eliminated prostitution. He mercilessly fought every form of over-emphasis on permissive public sex. The marriage age was raised to twenty-eight, and "social energy" was consciously used for ideological goals.

People with a healthy perception, who long for genuine freedom, have an angry aversion against the licentious destruction of human dignity. Since discipline gives a person more hope and freedom than libertarianism in the long run, communistic lands are relatively more attractive to people sensitive to moral purity than the degenerated West with its flood of sexual aggressions.

As a standard for the relationships of people, the "new morality" of the Western world is completely unsuited to physically and politically strong nations. Indeed, viewed more closely, our misuse of sexual energy proves to be a potentially devastating weapon for the destruction of our freedom. One day the Federal Republic of Germany will drop like a ripe fruit into the lap of a united East-West Germany, even though the Brandt regime solemnly declared such an East-West reunification "impossible." Here an old historical standard is repeated, namely, that a relaxation of sexual norms leads to such a weakening and softening of people that neighboring nations, morally and physically stronger, will one day regard this weakness as an invitation to come and take over by force. On the other hand, according to Unwin, "a people which, recognizing these standards, would be prepared consciously to observe sexual discipline for generations, giving equal right to husband and wife, could one day be capable of unimaginable cultural and spiritual accomplishments."

Furthermore, the isolation of sex pleasure in Western cultures must destroy the inner perception of the human spirit through which God contacts the person or by which man can be "inspired." The misuse of creative energies dulls the inner spiritual capacity for vision. Only a person whose motives, urges, thoughts and actions are directed in harmony with the Source of light becomes transparent to divine light. We are as capable of responding to higher impulses and inspirations as our smallest cell is capable of responding to the higher impulses of our spirit and will. But sexual corruption makes us incapable of responding to higher inspirations.

Jesus said that the pure of heart will see God. When the inner eye is bright and pure it is capable of perceiving the inner light of God. "And if your light is darkness, how deep will the darkness be!" (Matthew 6:23). Great will the darkness be when a whole nation destroys its ability to perceive inner truth! The knowledge and experience voiced throughout the Bible are scientifically confirmed by the research of I. D. Unwin.

Universally Binding Standards

An effort to find universally valid, absolute standards for human evolution, such as the effort put forth in this book, leads, on all levels, to the same conclusion. The ultimate standards are spiritual and moral. Through them the larger societal organisms, including those of tomorrow, are made possible. The moral standard, as idea and ideal, is absolute.

Reality, however, only approaches that ideal. For example, traffic regulations could be worked out to mathematical perfection. But these regulations are never followed with mathematical perfection. Nevertheless, because of this imperfection, it would not occur to anyone to agitate for the abandonment of the absolute standard of orderly traffic.

In recalling the early development of transportation we find that the rules were very indefinite and crude in the beginning. But these rules were not abandoned when they no longer served contemporary needs. They were either refined or replaced by better standards. Similarly, the above-mentioned points of orientation for moral standards needed today do not abandon old norms but either refine them or replace them. A condition of normlessness is not progressive; it is seriously regressive. Social dissolution is not a higher stage of evolution. But an advancement of standards for a higher societal organism is a higher stage of life.

Such societal organisms are the family, parish, business, school, community, city, state and nation in a world which has become increasingly condensed. To summarize once again: every community can be destroyed by dishonesty, fraud, thievery, calumny and flattery because these create mistrust and fear, making genuinely constructive cooperation impossible. A lively exchange of feelings, needs, ideas and materials is possible only in a society without "iron curtains." A balanced openness and transparency toward one's fellows imply *absolute honesty* as a moral standard. This standard is the basic requirement for all positive communication and for shared life in community.

Purity and transparency are as necessary to a well-ordered society as to a glass crystal. A crystal is transparent only when the structures of its molecules are parallel. Such a crystal is most capable of receiving light. When our drives and motives are parallel to one another, or harmoniously moving in the same direction, we are most capable of receiving truth and of living harmoniously in society.

We recognize impurity not only as a problem of hygiene but also of the emotions, motives and actions. Spiritual impurity appears in financial, sexual or political exploitation of others. Such misuse of others destroys the higher meaning of a neighbor's life as well as his destiny in a greater whole. Bitterness, hatred, frustration and disappointment are the unhappy results. On the other hand, drives and energies directed toward creative tasks do not revolt against each other; rather, they raise each other to a higher level. Thus, purity is the source of genuine progress.

Absolute purity is the standard for all higher living. Even on the lowest level, the more an organism's structures and functions are purified, the healthier it is. In the relationship between husband and wife, before and during marriage, and in every other human community, purity represents the basic principle of every lasting societal organism. This is certain, in spite of all psychological accusations made against the virtue of chastity. Other absolute standards are selflessness and loving responsibility toward others.

Images for these norms are healthy body cells. The healthy cell serves the greater whole selflessly. The white blood corpuscle offers itself in the battle against bacilli and viruses. But the cancer cell lives only for itself. It poisons and drains the organism.

Just as electronics increases the capacity of modern technology for constructive accomplishments, so also do modern psychology and sociology increase our capacity for understanding and governing our own conduct. Thus, the discovery of the unconscious provides new insights into the mask-wearing aspects of our behavior. We are more aware of desires to exploit and use others, and more aware of fear, ambition or hatred in our motives. Here, too, the point of departure for all right living is total honesty with oneself and others. *Honest, pure, selfless love is certainly the greatest thing on earth.*

These generally valid, absolute standards of honesty, purity, selflessness and love are the moral foundations for the existence of every higher culture and every modern social organism. It is our task to make them known throughout the world as replacements for the relative customs and morals of previous times and for the irrelevant "situation ethics" of today.

Absolute Moral Standards from the Knowledge of Revelation

There is a foundation for human behavioral standards other than scientific-analytical knowledge, one which formed the life of European peoples before scientific knowledge existed. It is called the "knowledge of revelation," part of which is the law of Moses with its ten commandments. Historical studies have proven that the people of Israel survived for nearly two thousand years without an external civic organization because of the law of Moses.

As a result, Israel recently could form a strong and successful state of its own. Decisive for the law of Moses are its physical and moral demands for purity. These are requirements for the existence and maintenance of the first monotheistic belief in God in the history of mankind. We have no explanation for this law, except that it resulted from revealed knowledge. Scientific knowledge, as developed today, did not exist at that time.

With all our scientific knowledge, it was discovered only recently that the twelfth day after menstruation is the end of a woman's ovulation period, or the optimal point of fertility. The Mosaic law, without having examined hormones or microscopic sections, recognized this fact for three thousand years. The law allows sexual intercourse only on the twelfth day after the beginning of the menstrual period, thus assuring the best chance of conception. This recognition of the time of fertility, along with a previous eleven-day abstinence, served the best interests of having healthy children, since sudden spermatogenesis in the male was avoided.

A view opposing periodic abstinence, made recently by the Kennedy Institute for Bio-ethics and published by moral theologian Bernard Haering in various theological magazines, warns against aging sperm and ova which are supposed to cause an increased loss of zygotes in their early stages of development. On the one hand, this would corroborate the biblical law forbidding intercourse eleven days before ovulation, during which time such aged gametes cannot exist. On the other hand, one can assume that in normal maturation the vital sperm cells, which are not too old, move toward the egg cell more quickly than those which are only half alive.

Moreover, the well-known Austrian scientist Dr. Josef Roetzer of Voecklabruck, who has for years been occupied with natural family planning, writes that Haering depends on the works of Guerrero, who is in no way correct in his research. Proving the opposite of Guerrero's claims, Dr. Roetzer and his co-workers, during the last three decades, registered every pregnancy which occurred in marriages of couples living according to the methods of natural regulation of births. They found neither an increased spontaneous loss of zygotes or embryos, nor increased malformations. Haering asserts the contrary in order to renew his efforts to bring the encyclical *Humanae Vitae* into discredit.

Guerrero's research and that of the Kennedy Institute on which Haering depends, offer no sign of inquiry as to how many women who conceived while practicing "rhythm" (and who, after the absence of their menstrual period and the first shock of an unwanted pregnancy), made all possible efforts to bring on menstruation through saltwater baths, hot steam baths, rinsings, flushings, etc. It is known that precisely in the first four weeks of pregnancy the embryo can be easily harmed in this way. Since the above mentioned research gives no evidence of awareness on this crucial point, Roetzer, therefore, rightly calls the statements of Haering and of the Kennedy Institute "foolishness."

However, at the time of Christ, the old moral standards, as they were being practiced, no longer sufficed. An intensification of standards became necessary. As far as human relationships were concerned, explanations of the commandments had become broad and loose. At the same time, the cultural and economic prescriptions of the Mosaic law were interpreted very narrowly. Consequently, the order of values often was reversed or perverted by exaggerated formalism. People forgot that laws were made to serve a dignified society, rather than men existing for the sake of the law!

When Jesus proclaimed, "You shall love the Lord your God with your whole heart, with your whole soul, and with all your mind, and your neighbor as yourself" (Matthew 22:17) as the first and greatest commandment, He announced the correct order of values. This new order refined and expanded the behavioral norms for human relationships. By becoming, Himself, an absolute moral standard of love, Jesus perfected all the other standards of moral behavior.

The fifth commandment, "You shall not kill," was expanded to prohibit contempt, hatred, and degrading of others, as well as their destruction. One who regards another as a mentally-ill fool, without caring about that person, was declared guilty of "hell fire." The sixth commandment was expanded to prohibit not only adultery as such but also a desirous look and consequent lust. The idea of honesty in the seventh and eighth commandments was enlarged to include everything which could weaken or mask a firm yes or no. When he said, "Take up your cross and follow me," Christ demanded a perfect readiness to replace human egoism with the will of God.

The standards of absolute honesty, purity, selflessness and love exist in the depths of human nature. Moses, the prophets, Christ, Paul and many others did not create these norms; they simply revealed them to others. As the great men of science revealed the laws of relationship between electrons and atoms, cells and organs, Moses and Jesus revealed laws of relationships between persons. Because these laws exist in nature we find substantial agreement between the norms of Christian, Jewish, Buddhist and other great world religions.

Modernizing the Penal Law

In an age of instant communication by means of radio, television, film and press, ideas of a "universal sense of morality" and a sense of shame are no longer regarded as relevant moral principles. With emphasis on the subjective approach this "universal sense of morality" can be weakened so quickly in the modern situation that it will not remain the same during the course of a single year.

Because a progressive spiritual paralysis can occur in people without their knowing it, clear objective norms are necessary to protect them from such a paralysis. Scientific research, in the best sense of the word, is needed for a correct "reform" of objective norms. If we are not to be ruled by the subjective values or one-sided ideologies of the mass media and power politics, we need scientifically refined objective standards of modern life.

The contemporary notion that relativistic customs and morals of the past should be discarded and that "freedom of conscience for the citizen who is of age" must be afforded through lawlessness is a dangerous illusion. Have promoters of this notion never thought about the fact that conscience functions only through clear moral standards? Don't they realize that only those individuals come of age who freely affirm such standards for the sake of the common order of life? He who wants to be a law unto himself and who regards moral laws as repressive, authoritarian and fascistic is still in his spiritual puberty and has the conscience of a child. How would a state maintain its system of taxation if it relegated the payment of taxes to the free choice of conscience? Likewise with business, political and cultural morality!

If the truth about behavioral standards can be recognized by scientific knowledge as well as by the knowledge of revelation and if both reveal essentially the same standards, then that truth has a universal character. Conscience must be orientated to this universal truth, otherwise individual and social development will be impossible.

Since certain forms of behavior, then, are socially disruptive, there must be a point at which lawful punishment is necessary. For example, when a lie becomes a deceit that directly harms another it should be punished. Formerly, adultery was punished because the destruction of a marriage and family is seriously harmful to the welfare of others. But when common welfare no longer is regarded as more important than individual happiness, punishments for violations of society are dismissed. In this way the protection of a whole nation is abandoned to individual exploiters and ideological deceivers. Then, indeed, one can be simultaneously so sentimental and schizophrenic that one readily sacrifices the lives of millions of unborn human beings to extorting money-hungry doctors, but at the same time makes a hellish noise when a criminal or mass-murderer is not treated "with kid gloves."

Whoever is willing to see a glimmer of reality must recognize that the loss of clear moral standards results in total ideological and political confusion and automatically leads to anarchy and social dissolution. If this confusion and rejection of moral standards penetrate not only the state but also the churches, then every hope of renewal seems to be in vain. According to the Bible, it is a situation ripe for God's wrath and punishment.

The so-called *Statement of Sex Ethics* of the EKD is a classic example of today's confusion of minds.[34] In this *Statement*, the last of all clear moral norms are abandoned. The concepts of sin and guilt, of grace and forgiveness, are completely excluded from the sexual realm and replaced by empty psychological platitudes. When the standard of purity is relaxed in favor of any possible kind of sexual partnership, such as finds its meaning only in mutual pleasure and no longer in the existence of new life, one can imagine what happens to the church.

Finally, it becomes clear to anyone who allows himself the perception how decisive was Pope Paul's refusal — in the encyclical *Humanae Vitae* — to co-operate in the universal sex trend. We ought to be immensely grateful to him for remaining constant in spite of enormous pressures from all directions.

Part Three

The Encyclical *Humanae Vitae*

The Concept of "Nature" in *Humanae Vitae*

During recent decades a shift of emphasis has taken place in judgments about the meaning of human sexuality. Previously, sex was understood in the light of the creation of new human life. This shift of emphasis has been in the direction of the individual's subjective feelings, "happiness" and complete sexual satisfaction. The purpose of this shift was to proclaim a fundamental right of each individual, married or single, to a "happy sexual life."

A decisive contribution to this development was made by the Swiss psychiatrist Theodor Bovet in his book on marriage, *Das Geheimnis ist gross*. In this book much is said about the "mystery of erotic sexual love," but practically nothing is said about the still greater "mystery" of the origin of human life, the essence of which no one has been able to explain to this day. Bovet strongly emphasizes the emotions experienced by the marriage partners in sexual union. This was a new emphasis for Christians at that time. Therefore, many welcomed the book as a liberating force. Others warned Bovet of its consequences. But he failed to listen. Holding to his original view, he subsequently defended contraception, premarital sex, and homosexuality. He furnished important arguments for all those who were interested in disregarding former sex standards. Like the Bible, his book is presented to newly married couples even today in many Protestant churches.[35]

Similarly, a shift of emphasis from the objective purpose of sex to the subjective experience of sex has occurred among Catholic moral theologians in their discussion of the hierarchy of marital values. The question as to which value — procreation, the rearing of children, the marriage partnership, joy, bodily beauty or carnal pleasure — should be regarded as the most important one from which all others flow, became central to the discussions. In this theological context, Pope Paul VI's *Humanae Vitae*, affirming the basic objective value of the marital act, came as a jolt. And it was met by raging dissent.

The main attack by all the opponents of *Humanae Vitae* was

directed against its concept of "nature." Many critics understood "nature" to mean the biological aspect of the human person, which they thought to be similar to the biology of animals.

In *Stimmen der Zeit*, the biologist and behaviorist Wolfgang Wickler, also a critic of *Humanae Vitae*, tried to determine the essence of human sexuality from the behavior of animals, without regard to the unique biological or spiritual aspects of human nature.[36] According to Wickler, such a consideration of biological laws must "lead to an entirely different view regarding the marriage act from the one which Pope Paul had." If "nature" is the regulative principle, thinks Wickler, it must be possible to define it by comparing it with behavioral patterns in animals. By observing the part of physical nature which human beings have in common with animals, it should be possible to arrive at general conclusions for laws pertaining to all creatures.

Wickler regards this project as altogether possible because sex processes are common to all living beings. He believes he can show that the formation of a partnership and mating are two different things which are related, but which can also occur separately. He maintains that on the level of biological nature, sexual union for propagation and sexual union for the formation of a partnership are goals distinct from each other and separately attainable. In this way he tries to attack the encyclical, which demands an inseparable connection between sexual union and propagation.

Wickler says, "One can perform the marital act out of love for a partner with a definite plan for a child. However, one can also perform it, without regard to offspring, solely for the purpose of reciprocal union. The consummation of both of these acts is different in quality and distinct; and neither will be experienced as less meaningful." Both of these marital acts, then, are different subjective experiences. He continues, "Since they are distinct and each has its own value, it follows that not every marital act needs to be performed for the purpose of creating life in order to be permissible. If, however, personal love and surrender were of a higher value than the creation of new life, they would have to be the goal of every marital act."

According to Wickler, "complete continence over a long period of time" contradicts the essence of the marital union. He holds that "permanent continence and the limiting of sexual intercourse to times before or after the wife's fertile periods are unnatural, making the conjugal union and the attainment of the final goal of marriage difficult. Such things, however, are forbidden by the natural law, according to St. Thomas Aquinas."

Driven by Instinct? Directed by Knowledge?
Guided by God?

One could say to Wickler's argument that any attempt to deduce human values from biological patterns of animals is false. The Old Testament purposely uses the word "know" to describe the sex relationship between husband and wife. Human knowledge constitutes the main difference between the nature of human and animal sexuality. The animal is driven by instinct. It does not "know" the meaning of its sexual relationships. In the animal the sexual impulse does not originate in consciousness but in instinctual responses to certain odors and colors.

Human sexuality, on the other hand, is consciously experienced. The human being can arouse sex through his imagination, repress it, sublimate it, transform it, and become neurotic through repression or excessive expression. Human sexuality is not purely instinctive, but rather is affirmed or denied. Therefore, it must become integrated into the total personality and controlled by a sense of responsibility.

To "know" implies conscious awareness of the partner in his or her total sexuality and individuality. It means understanding the inner being of the loved partner and all aspects of the love relationship, including its creative task, its indissolubility and full responsibility to the partner, to the children and to God. To "know" also includes an awareness of modern scientific research, which shows that the child is the synthesis of parental heritage, an entirely new human being who can never again be returned to the original hereditary factors. Marital "knowledge" of the proper order of values in human sexuality is necessary not only for the good of children but also for the good of the partners. Thus the individual realizes that his personal "right to a happy sex life" in no way is the "pre-eminent" or highest value of marriage. He realizes that the greatest mystery of marriage, the creation of new human life, is its supreme value.

To "know" a wife, then, implies the opposite of being "driven by instinct," or "reacting blindly." It is much more an action which embraces total human consciousness and responsibility as well as unconscious feelings and emotions. In other words, it embraces the total humanity of the person. How, then, can human sexuality be reduced to the level of animal sexuality? Sexual behavior patterns, externally similar in both human beings and animals, undergo a fundamental "change of function" in human beings from blind instinct to conscious knowing.

Unity and Synchronization in Human Sexuality

Through the power to know, a human being can discern the specific sexual processes and use them as he chooses. Thus, the creation of new human life is consciously sought in only a small number of sexual relations. But a sexual act which does not intentionally destroy its procreative purpose is basically different from one which radically excludes the procreative purpose.

Some critics of *Humanae Vitae*, like Helmut Koester, recognize the goal-orientated unity of all biological processes in human sexuality. In an article in *Stimmen der Zeit*, Koester says:

> Ovulation, fertilization and the implantation of the fertilized egg are very complicated processes. They are prepared for in pre- and post-ovulatory phases by a whole network of daily and hourly changing biochemical reactions, impulses to growth and conditions of development in the 'tween-brain-hypophysis systems, the ovaries, the oviduct, the womb, indeed, in the entire body of the woman. The exact functioning of every part of these complex processes, and especially the perfect synchronization of all of them during and after ovulation, are necessary so that their final purpose, namely, ovulation, fertilization and the implantation of the fertilized egg, can take place. The precision of these complex processes, which occur monthly between two menstruations, remind one who must analyze them of the complexity, synchronization and precision of numerous smaller parts during the count-

down of well-known technical undertakings which are arranged for, and directed to, one specific goal. Such a goal cannot be reached if even just one small part fails to function. Similarly, all smaller functions are directed to the goal of ovulation, fertilization and the implantation of the fertilized egg. Failure in synchronization by just hours can suffice to cause failure in attaining the final goal.[13]

Koester insists that the principle of correct timing in biological processes may be interrupted by the new contraceptives. Other critics of the encyclical also insisted upon this point. Thus, the Family Planning Commission of Catholic doctors in Germany, along with a group of Catholic doctors from Freiburg, published strong stands against the encyclical in the *German Medical Periodical*, No. 35/68 and 36/68.[37] However, these critics showed their incredibility when they mistakenly said that the "marital act" is considered "the same as procreation in the encyclical." It is an intentional distortion of facts to suggest that the psychological attitude of readiness to accept a child (an attitude which the encyclical demands) is the same thing as biological reproduction.

The expression "interruption of synchronization" used by Koester and his colleagues is an active, deliberate change in biological processes. However, other methods based on timing (temperature and mucus observation) are not an active, deliberate effort to change biological synchronization. These methods require a "knowing" of the natural hiatus in synchronization. They respect the fertility of the woman as a gift, instead of violating this fertility for the sake of sexual pleasure.

Natural and Unnatural Family Planning

When it becomes clear that the factor of uncertainty in the temperature method is no greater than that in the use of the "pill," and that the temperature method has no harmful side effects, the question of "natural" and "unnatural" becomes very relevant.[38] If continence is maintained three days beyond the end of ovulation, natural methods are equally as effective as the "pill." In the meantime, the great harm which comes from a prolonged use of the "anti-baby pill" has been publicized in spite of all the counter propaganda by its paid champions. Among these effects are count-less thromboses, a large number of deaths from embolisms even among younger women, harm to the liver and digestive glands, skin trouble, eye problems, physical changes, danger to metabo-lism, and hardening of the ovaries to the point of hereditary harm caused by chromosomal breaks in the egg cells. (Results of these breaks appear only in the third or fourth generation because they are recessive.) These numerous physical problems clearly show that the "pill" does not have anywhere near the medical advan-tage of natural methods.

In this connection, it is rewarding to read the books of Dr. E. Sievers, *Natur und Enzyklika, Wege zur naturgemaessen Empfaengnisregelung* and *Empfaengnisregelung und andere Sexu-alprobleme*, which were published in 1969, 1970 and 1972, respec-tively, by the Johann Wilhelm Verlag in Wuerzburg. The medical aspect of birth control methods is presented with such great care by this author that married couples can follow them safely.

Beyond the biological differences between the "pill" and natural methods, there is a psychological difference that should be decisive for theological consideration.

Psychological-Moral Distinctions

Surprisingly, the psychological difference between the natural and drug methods of birth control did not appear in the majority reports of the papal commission on family planning. The abstinence required by the natural methods has great psychological and moral significance. A special quality of responsible awareness appears in one who prefers to abstain from the marital act instead of ex-pecting a partner to take harmful "pills" for the sake of enjoying sexual pleasure at will. Those who are not sexually disciplined cannot make such a moral decision. How can they accept the tem-porary or even prolonged periods of continence at times demanded by love, for physical or other reasons, in every marriage?

Promoters of chemical and artificial contraceptives, such as Wickler, Koester and others, maintain that abstinence at the time of ovulation is a psychological mistake. They hold that ovulation is the time when most women are hormonally and physically most ready for sexual intercourse.

That may be true. However, the pill mutilates the very same hormonal condition which makes women more disposed for sexual intercourse. Therefore, critics of abstinence are being dishonest. The same critics have no objection to sexual relations after menopause, when a woman's sexual hormones are greatly reduced. However, the mental factor in the sexuality of woman plays at least as great a role as the hormonal factor.[39]

There are women who become frigid from using the "pill." Very likely this results as much from the "pills'" hormonal disruption as from the husband's pressure on her to abuse her nature. Many men believe they have a perfect right to marital relations at any time, and that their wife must comply with their wishes. Because of their husband's lack of consideration and restraint, these women are driven to an ever-stronger resistance. Feeling themselves degraded to the level of a plaything, they might begin to experience disgust for all sex, and even neurosis. In connection with my discussion with the SPD minister of justice and the group in charge of pornography in the Federal Republic of Germany, I received a large number of letters from women saying how the combination of the "pill" and the promotion of sex through pornography had destroyed their marriages.

On the other hand, women who freely choose the "pill" do not want to take it in vain. They want to compensate for the inconvenience by increasing their sexual pleasure. As a result they become sexually aggressive or excessive; they demand too much from their husbands, lose erotic charm and, thus, disgust their husbands. Actually, many women, in one way or another, experience a negative change of personality because of the "pill." The effects eventually are disturbing to a marriage, and certainly, also, to the married couple's relationship with God. At such a point of disorientation it is difficult for a couple to judge whether the use of the "pill" is right or wrong, or whether they have been deceived by false propaganda. It is totally irresponsible for the Church and the theologians to abandon such couples to their own "moral judgments," and to blame them for the consequences that usually follow, instead of giving them clear standards and moral guidance.

In this connection it was extremely interesting to hear numerous reports favorable to the temperature and cervical mucus methods at a national conference on Natural Family Planning (St. John's University, Collegeville, Minnesota, June, 1974.) Those married couples who changed from using the "pill" to natural family planning unanimously reported positive effects on their marriage. Marriage counselors reported the same good results.

When a woman knows her own fertile and infertile periods, it is possible to see the effects in her personality. In the knowledge of her special and unique ability to become a mother, she seems to experience greater self-appreciation. (Knowing the periods of fertility assures the possibility of motherhood.) On the other hand, by temporarily or permanently using "pills" or by having an operation, certain personality values seem to recede in a woman. According to all known laws of psychology, striking personality changes are unavoidable.

The Bible and Contraception

Those who insist that there is nothing in the Bible about contraception and birth control purposely misinterpret the condemnation of Onan (Gen. 38:10). They say that Onan was condemned because he disobeyed the law that exhorted him to give his dead brother a child. What about the method he used? Onan was condemned also for "spilling his seed upon the ground."

Also in the Old Testament, the days directly after a woman's period, as mentioned before, were a time of abstinence in order to achieve the best chance of fertilization (Lev. 38:28). At the time of Christ, these laws and prescriptions were entirely acceptable and uncontested. Jesus never questioned them, as He did other laws of the Old Testament.

Millions of Jewish married couples, inasmuch as they were orthodox, law-abiding Jews, have lived according to these laws for three thousand years. Thus they have demonstrated that the precept of continence contained in the law was practiced for nearly half the time of the female cycle and was in no way inhuman or impossible. The British journalist Phyllis Bowman, who herself comes from such a family, told me that statistics prove traditional Jewish marriages have the lowest percentage of divorces.

Love Responds to Life

In her book *Love Responds to Life*, the American author Mary Rosera Joyce develops several ideas on the human power to give life, which I would like to quote at length.[40]

> The relationship between the coital act and its power to give life is not one that is external, like the relation between hand and glove, or one that can be put on or taken off at will. It is a relationship as deep within the being of the person as that between his act of listening and his power to hear. By willfully separating a freely chosen action from one of its fully human powers, the person denies the unity of his being . . . .
>
> In defining the sterilization of persons, nothing need be said about physical organs or procedures of any kind. The way it is done is not what it is! Human sterilization is an external separation of coital union (a personally chosen act of communication) from its power to give life. All forms of contraception are *included* in this general definition. Since the regulation of conception by periodic continence is not a direct impairment of the power to give life, it is not an internal separation of any kind, and is *excluded* from the definition of sterilization.
>
> Periodic continence is a way of avoiding the fertility that is actually there. All forms of contraception, on the other hand, reduce fertility to temporary sterility. Though periodic continence and contraception may be used for the same purpose, so that a child will not be conceived, this same purpose does not make them the same thing . . . .
>
> In persons, induced sterility is not just an interruption of a biological process, as it is in animals, but an interruption of his entire being as a person. People may say that their feelings have not been affected, but the being of a person is not identical with his feelings. People may say that their self-awareness has not been affected, but the being of a person is not identical with his self-awareness. What the person does to his *being as a person* is known by his subconscious mind, even if it is "happily" blocked out or ignored by his conscious mind.
>
> One human act projecting an internal separation into another human act is a way of taking a willful stand against the unity of one's total person. When this is done by people for the sake of

their union with each other, their love is in question. If one person does not receive the unity of his own being in love, how can he receive the being of another person in love?

In order to prevent the emotional disturbance of continence, people resort to the much deeper disturbance of contraception. But no one is honest who refuses to admit what he is doing to the unity of his being for the sake of his emotional unity with another person. Anyone who admits what he is doing will not repress it or block it out of his mind. He will remain uneasy with contraception. Formerly, people became sick by repressing guilt. Though the practice of contraception is not necessarily an instance of psychic neurosis, it is a kind of deeper, ontological neurosis. And, as Carl Jung said, 'neurosis is a substitute for legitimate suffering.' From the point of view of the person's emotional life, any form of willfully sterilized intercourse might be regarded as normal, understandable behavior in some cases. But from the point of view of the person's being, this behavior is profoundly unnatural . . . .

The separation that the person imposes within his being by forcefully reducing fertility to sterility is one of deforming, rather than of altering, his power to give life. He tries to reduce to the level of biology something that is much more than biological in nature. And since the human power to give life is an interpersonal power, one that is realized by two persons acting together, a devaluation of this power by one of these persons is also a devaluation of this power in the other person. Contraception is a debasing not only of their shared power to give life, but also of the sexual act from which this power is internally separated, and ultimately of the very being of both persons involved.

Attitudes Make a Difference

Natural methods often have been called forms of contraception. This is incorrect. The attitude of most married couples who use a natural method remains "open to the birth of a child." But the attitude of couples where the wife takes "anti-baby pills" is most often anti-baby, that is, opposed to a child.

The difference between the two becomes clear when, in spite of the method, a child is conceived. Couples who used a natural method almost always accept the child as God's gift to them. However, those who have a child in spite of artificial contraceptives, or in spite of the "unfailing pill," usually retain a negative attitude toward the child. Thus, the tendency to seek an abortion is greater in "pill" users.

Promoters of the "pill" repeatedly refer to the large number of children born in spite of natural methods. But the real reason for the birth of these children is that, in most cases, temperatures were not taken, nor mucus examined. This is not an argument against the natural method as such, but against the so-called "decisions of conscience" of married couples, who tell themselves and everyone else that for social, financial or physical reasons they absolutely cannot have one more child. Yet when a child does come, they accept the situation. Most often they are even happy to have the child. Such children who cost parents the most are regarded, later on, as the greatest blessings. Most of these parents say they cannot understand why they did not want the child in the first place. From this it is easy to see how flexible many consciences are, how changeable and manageable by mass propaganda they become. The need conscience has for simple, absolute guides remains clear.

It is naive to believe that the normal "conscience" is completely unaffected by the trends and propaganda of the times. When conscience is being offered flexible, complicated, relative psycho-moral rules understandable only by a few intellectuals and changeable according to the situation, brainwashing results. Comforting explanations for contraception made by the majority of the papal commissioners, e.g., that "the virtue of purity would be promoted" or that "great educational benefit would be derived," have had to be retracted long since. In the light of the actual sex trends of our times, it is plain to see that Pope Paul VI made the right decision.

Wanted Children

The new idea one hears repeatedly, even in churches today, is that only wanted children should be born. This idea is used as an argument for abortion. Martin Luther well might have turned in his grave when such articles appeared in the Lutheran monthly.[41] Naturally, the child that is prayed for and consciously wanted is the Christian's ideal goal in "family planning according to God's plan." Something entirely different, however, is the "wanted child" of egoistic parents who prevent the birth of subsequent children through the use of contraceptives or abortion. The egoism of such parents is transferred directly to the "wanted children." In fact, it increases to the extent that these children become puppets or tyrants who are later cursed by their parents. Many of them become unhappy creatures, incapable of handling themselves in society. This situation is worse for the child than the fate of the child not wanted at first but later accepted as a gift from God.

The Counter-Evolution of Abortion

In the statement of the medical doctors of Ulm, as early as 1964, we called attention to the fact that public propaganda for "anti-baby pills," with the subsequent increase of public and private sex, is not a suitable remedy for combating the abortion epidemic. At first, abortion statistics seemed to disprove this prognosis. Research showed that contraceptive use caused the number of abortions to decline at first, so that there seemed to be no reason to push for abortion upon request. However, the modern "democratic" claim that we have a right to the greatest possible sexual satisfaction and pleasure, first promoted along with the "anti-baby pill," soon resulted in a demand for total abortion freedom. The subsequent increased number of abortions ultimately negated initial contraceptive "successes." Thus, our prediction is proven correct.

The assertion thoughtlessly spread by governments, as well as by many theologians today, that abortion is a concern of women alone, simply ignores the child's right to life. Only because of the child's presence is the question of abortion raised in the first place. The father's right to protect his child and the doctor's duty to protect life also are ignored. Likewise eliminated from consideration is God's right to the life and love of His creature.

As early as six years after the encyclical, the abortion trend was in full swing. The possibility that such a trend would develop was completely overlooked by those who believed it necessary to make certain concessions to the spirit of the times. They thought these concessions were needed lest theologians appear too old-fashioned and reactionary, and lest too many of the faithful would be lost. As a result, the pornography used in illustrated magazines, films and television was no longer regarded as retrogressive. And the idea of promoting abortion, which was completely unthinkable even five years ago, is today thought to be acceptable. By a similar process of retrogression, the guards and executioners of the concentration camps became accustomed to killing Jewish children. At first this duty made them ill.

Crossing the Rubicon to Complete Sexual "Freedom"

Exactly as Pope Paul indicated, the crossing of the Rubicon — from natural methods of conception regulation to radical technological prevention of conception — led to sexual license. Between these two types of methods is a heavy dividing line — a biological, psychological, moral, and religious dividing line — between a "yes" of openness and an absolute "no" to a child. This point, at which there is a complete isolation of sexual pleasure from total sexuality, is the crucial point of initiation for the sexual counter-evolution.

The consequences ruin civilizations, churches and cultures. When some theologians try to control the surge of sex by forbidding a few things, making rules for special cases, admonishing to chastity, no one pays attention. In the meantime, the storm against celibacy is nothing more than an off-shoot of the sex revolution. This storm originates not with the question of a priest's spiritual call, but basically from the desire for sexual pleasure. The sex propaganda becomes so loud that priests no longer want, or are able, to resist.

Human Sexual Nature Is Much More than the Sum of Animal Functions

We have already shown that the physical, chemical and biological laws of nature are valid on all levels of existence, including human life. Just as the cell exists on a higher level than all its electrons, atoms and molecules together, so a human being, as God's co-creator, is a higher level of being than animals. In no way can this be explained from the sum total of man's animal-like components and urges. The whole is greater than the mere sum of its parts. Whatever is true of a human being as a whole is also true of the nature of human sexuality.

If one is not prepared to respect the higher quality of a human being, then one makes the unhappy mistake of simply transferring laws of nature from the animal to the human level, thus falsifying the essence of the human being. Adolf Hitler, mercilessly proclaiming the right of the stronger over the weaker as a natural right, presents an example of an animal concept of man. Hoping to achieve a pure race, he divided human life into biological and racial values. But with this frame of mind, he led Germany and Europe into a world catastrophe costing millions of human lives. The same kind of false transference is involved in applying to human sexuality the distinction in some animals between reproduction and sexuality, pairing and propagation. The consequence is the disintegration of entire nations and cultures. Thus, norms recognized in the behavior of animals often accomplish the exact opposite when taken as guides for human behavior.

Perversion of the Value Scale Leads to Perversion of Sexuality

By evaluating the enjoyment of love higher than the creation of new human life and absolutizing the isolation of sex from procreation, one establishes "increased sexual pleasure" as a "fundamental right to a happy sex life." [42] The automatic result of this position is that every form of "increased sexual pleasure" is regarded as an "equal *right* to a happy sex life." Not only the legislators but also the churches have drifted in the direction of equalizing all forms of sex pleasure. Thus, the new Catholic Dutch Catechism [17] as well as the EKD [34] statement on sex ethics no longer recognize masturbation as sinful. And homosexuality is regarded as a special situation which must be respected if it "does not harm the partnership."

The specific result of this perversion of values on the sex education of the young, from kindergarten to college, is psychological and moral chaos. For many families the result is catastrophe. What young person will ever realize that this "right to increased sexual pleasure" may be enjoyed only in marriage, for which a legal certificate from the register of marriages is needed! If premarital chastity is considered an old-fashioned, impossible repression coming from old societal structures and ecclesiastical prudery, the young will feel encouraged to become promiscuous and thus incapable of sustaining the permanent commitment of married life.

Whoever believes he can be effective in changing this trend by conducting sex education in the kindergarten and elementary school is sadly deceived. Such a one is like a teacher who expects his ten-year-old pupils to learn about traffic violations by making them memorize the parts of a car and by explaining the function of driving while he raves about the excitement of speed, saying, "Now you know everything about it, but you must wait until you are eighteen to get a driver's license."

Everyone knows that this type of education is no remedy against traffic violations and accidents, but a temptation to drive prematurely. Why should it be any different with sex education in schools? Early sex education about contraceptives, the technique of sex, etc., is instruction for reckless premarital sexual intercourse and, for that reason, cannot be called sex education, but a forced awakening of the need for sex in the young. The best sex education is given to children only by their parents. If it is given in schools, the factual material has to be incorporated into the total realm of life's values.

A year before the encyclical *Humanae Vitae*, I approached Professor Boeckle, chief exponent of the free use of the "pill," and explained to him that the isolation of sexual pleasure from procreation would make it impossible to educate the unmarried in discipline, chastity and the transformation of sexual energy. He disputed this point. But the results of his thinking are well known today, and have precipitated an unprecedented educational crisis. The theory of Wilhelm Reich, that the way to social revolution is the way of sexual revolution, is being proven true in our high schools and colleges.[11]

Clearly, then, one must consider the totality of human sexuality with all its ramifications if one wishes to avoid catastrophic mistakes. The "scientific" fragmentation of human knowledge, which makes some scientists "specialty idiots," is explosively dangerous in questions of sexuality. Whoever judges human sexuality solely from the standpoint of individual happiness, while excluding the development of spiritual and moral character, will experience catastrophe in his own family. A parent has authority to recommend premarital chastity to his children only if he himself, for love of his children, practices periods of continence in his own marriage. Youth learns from life as it is lived. In cases where the children know their mother takes "pills," what example do they have for premarital discipline? Indeed, it is no longer possible.

Upon seeing this result as a fact, an American educator, Peter Riga, withdrew his signature from the Catholic University's published declaration against *Humanae Vitae*. In the October, 1973, issue of the periodical *Triumph*, he described his reasons, expressed his regret and apologized publicly.[43] (The article is printed at the end of this book as Appendix III).

Further Views about the "Nature" of Human Sexuality

It is surprising that Wickler and other researchers produce no example from animals when they argue against continence and for contraception.[36] Wickler maintains that "longer periods of continence are unnatural in marriage," indeed, even forbidden, according to St. Thomas Aquinas, who says it is "against the natural law." Examples from animal life must convince Wickler of the opposite. Crows and gray geese have permanent "marriages." These birds have long periods of "continence" and short periods of sexual activity, but their "marriages" in no way suffer from their "continence."

Why, then, should partnership, family life and marriage in human beings depend on the practice of sex? Are human beings less capable of faithfulness than these birds? And what happens to those married couples who, for reasons of health, war, or prison terms must refrain from sexual intercourse for long periods, or even permanently? Is Homer's *Odyssey* not a classic example, although in no way Christian, of marital faithfulness without sex, indeed, of a deepening of the inner relationship through continence and perseverance during a time of tension?

In connection with the idea of nature in *Humanae Vitae* and of the "nature" of human sexuality, it is necessary to recall briefly two facts which were explained in the second part of this book.

It is certainly noticeable that only human beings have sex diseases. These exist only because they are spread by a promiscuous change of partners. Modern promiscuity has caused gonorrhea, which had almost died out, to become the most common infectious disease except for ordinary influenza. Likewise, syphilis, almost unheard of formerly, has again become a common disease. If one sees the ravaging results of these diseases, and considers that all natural laws have a higher meaning in human beings, one understands these diseases as a rebellion of nature against the promiscuity and sexual excesses in human beings.

Wickler ignored the most important biological point in the nature of the human being: the specifically human sign of virginity: the hymen. Certainly every biologist and scientist must ask himself why nature has provided, only in human beings, an anatomical difference between virgin and wife in the fold of skin which practically closes the vagina. This tissue has no biological meaning. Hygienically, it may cause cleanliness problems during the woman's period. Since all bodily organs and tissues have some purpose, the hymen, which lacks any animal meaning, must have a specifically human meaning.

Anyone who says the hymen is meaningless contradicts all the traditions of cultured peoples who deduced from this anatomical circumstance the singular quality of human sexual union. They always regarded injury done to virginity, outside a permanent marital union, as a serious offense against a woman's honor, dignity and personal integrity. The veneration of the Blessed Virgin Mary is no accidental part of Catholic belief. The Mother of Christ, more than any other, has been the image of dignity for the European woman during the past two thousand years. European culture would be unthinkable without her. Is it accidental that her image, which formerly dominated our villages and towns (in the middle ages the people of Ulm wanted to erect an eight-meter-high statue of the Mother of Christ on the pinnacle of the Ulm cathedral), is now replaced by pictures of prostitutes and partially nude women who give the impression that they are ready to disrobe entirely? Why have so many lost sight of the highest expression of womanliness which formed our mothers, enabling them to develop their personalities and to do unbelievably great things?

Dr. Wickler and his associates forgot the distinguishing biological marks of human sexuality. Their criticism of Pope Paul VI, that he failed "to concern himself with biological laws," therefore, reverts back to them.

In summary, the three aspects of human sexuality — procreative, unitive, and familial — seem like three branches of the same stem. Whoever wishes to separate one branch separates it from the common stem and root. Such a branch may bloom temporarily in a vase, but soon it wilts and dies.

The contemporary disintegration of the creativity of sex is an absolute proof for this threefold principle of integration in human sexuality. The breakdown appears in a swift decline in births as well as in cultural accomplishments; in the rapid rise in divorces; the deterioration of sexual joy as it is replaced by empty passion, disgust, and even suicide; the increase in perversions and sex diseases; the rise of political anarchy and the general de-humanization of multiple life situations. This total cultural disintegration should convince us that we have lost our way and that we should start over again with the full human truth about our sexual nature.

The Super-nature of Human Sexuality

In human sexuality there is not only a "nature" but also a "super-nature," the source of its transcendent meaning. When marriage, sexual union and procreation are regarded as gifts of God and as a decisive part of God's plan for personal life and family planning, love and joy are increased. For this reason Pope Paul VI speaks of the serious duty of married couples, who are free and responsible collaborators with God, to transmit human life, a task which is also a source of great joy to them. Whoever has tried to do this knows it is not merely pious talk, but one of life's greatest opportunities to cooperate with God.

I can understand that materialistic scientists would not consider the "nature" of human sexuality in reference to God. But I cannot understand Christian scientists who study human sexuality simply on the level of behavioral patterns in animals and who think that sexual pleasure is the highest value in human sexuality. Thus they rob human sexuality of its super-natural character and reduce God to a sentimental decoration of materialistic science.

In his encyclical, Pope Paul VI insists that the problem of births, like every other serious human problem, must be seen beyond all partial views — biological, psychological or sociological — in the light of human totality, natural and supernatural. To prevent human sexuality from being victimized by a one-sided or short-sighted view, Pope Paul studied all the documents he had received, and, after mature deliberation and ardent prayer, published his statement. Thus, he was far from considering biological nature alone, as some of his opponents who made this very mistake themselves have accused him. By "nature" Pope Paul did *not* mean the biological behavior of animals, but human "nature," created according to God's image. He saw the various components of human nature as having a divine origin and as receiving their ultimate meaning and norms from God. Thus, for him, the meaning of "nature" and "natural law" is different for human beings than for merely biological creatures.

Where there is no belief in man's creation according to God's image, it is not possible to determine the right type of family planning. This statement might make some readers angry. But a pure and humble child can understand it much better than a scientist whose inner receptivity to God is disturbed.

The Church and the Counsel of the Laity

A false dichotomy between religious and lay people has tended to separate the spiritual life from life in the world. Therefore less of the spiritual was expected from lay people. In fact, in many lay persons spiritual experiences were replaced by loyalty to the authority and laws of the Church. This absence of spirituality in the laity is a serious problem for the Pope and bishops today.

How could a lay Catholic scientist give good counsel to the Pope on questions of human life if this scientist was not a spiritually developed person? It is not surprising that scientifically trained lay people would judge the question of birth control from their own physiological and medical viewpoints, and recognize no real significance in spiritual and religious aspects of the question.

On the contrary, we need a double-eyed understanding. Whoever for six days out of the week views the world with the eye of scientific objectivity and relativity and tries to use the other eye on Sunday should not be surprised if the power of his Sunday eye is weak. He should understand that he is not seeing with both eyes simultaneously, and thus he fails to have the necessary depth of focus. His condition of double vision causes "dizziness and headaches."

Lay people who have never learned to see both the inner and outer dimensions of reality or who cannot integrate science and revelation are in no mental condition for counselling the Church. Lay people who have the undeveloped faith of children, along with the most updated scientific knowledge, necessarily must offer the Pope and bishops materialistic counsel. It is no wonder, then, that such counsel would not be taken seriously in any ultimate way, because it would destroy faith in God.

The Limits of Science

It is impossible to discover the true being of another person, or to prove the existence of oneself, through scientific analysis alone. Rather, we experience ourselves and each other only as living persons. In spite of all possible psychoanalysis, the self transcends the grasp of science. Scientific, analytical methods, by their very essence, are unsuited for exploring the mystery of spiritual existence.

Therefore, when anyone approaches the question of contraception from purely psychological-sociological or medical-biological points of view, ignoring the spiritual-religious dimensions of this question, they use only one eye. The "scientific eye" without the "eye of faith" lacks the necessary depth of vision. Thus, the Christian scientist comes of age only when he lives with God and places his life and his knowledge under God's direction. He remembers the words: "If I speak with the tongues of angels, but do not have love, I am a noisy gong, a clanging cymbal. If I have the gift of prophecy and, with full knowledge, comprehend all mysteries; if I have faith great enough to move mountains, but have not love, I am nothing!" (1 Cor. 13:1 ff.).

Are we not perishing today because of scientific haughtiness? Science is being exploited when it is used to rationalize false assumptions, to promote one-sided ideologies and to liquidate human life. Without the proper vision, psycho-scientific methods can have a brain-washing effect, and physical-chemical knowledge can destroy the earth.

Naturally, it is highly desirable to refine our scientific knowledge and methods and to use them in the service of our fellow man. But what we need, above all else, is a clear knowledge of our own position in relation to God. We need to affirm our role in bringing all creation to Him.

The Degeneration of Confession

"Admission and confession of sin" ought to be a source of genuine renewal for both individuals and community. But the real meaning of confession — a reconciliation between God and man — gradually has been lost. More and more it became a self-centered concern for personal salvation. The idea of the Kingdom of God, at one time the spiritual and ideological foundation of the West, had been compromised to such an extent by Pope-emperor rivalries that the sense of Christian community was harmed. The words of Jesus (Matthew 6:33), "Seek first the Kingdom of God and his justice, and all else will be added to you" were forgotten. In this vacuum, people began to ask, "How do *I* find a merciful God?

Through faith, or through good works?" As a result, a genuine transformation of creative energies into activity for the building of the Kingdom was not sufficiently possible.

The Real Meaning of Confession

According to its original meaning, Confession is not only the subjective unburdening of sin, but also, and much more, the objective restoration of a destroyed relationship between God and man. A sick, lame or poisoned member of the community (organism) is healed again. Eleven times St. Paul uses the image of the physical body to clarify spiritual realities. We too may use this image once again to clarify the spiritual reality of Confession.

Thus, Confession resembles the annihilation of bacteria and viruses. Such a process is necessary for keeping bodily members properly conditioned to receive and respond to directive impulses given by the spirit. Poisoned cells become weak and incapable of reacting. Cancer cells are incapable of receiving impulses from higher structures. When the members of an organism no longer are sensitive to its superior control, the notion develops that no such superior control exists; anarchy is the end result.

Continuing this comparison further, the problem of experiencing God's existence in modern society is not intellectual or scientific. It is a problem basically involving the degree of purification of "cells" and "organs," so that these members might respond to the guiding ideal or regulative laws in the "nucleus." A healthy conscience is a necessary condition for individual readiness to perceive divine impulses and meaningful directives.

Modern atheism and nihilism, even in large materialistic countries, is not a scientific problem; it is the after-effect of destroyed directive power in the core of personality. When this directive power is lost, conscience is relativized, and the perception "antennae" that detect God's plan go dead. Healing, or the restoring of the ability to experience God's presence once again, is not possible without spiritual detoxification. Forgiveness of sin is the decisive prerequisite for a renewed partnership with God in God's plan for the world. The true test of forgiveness and absolution is not only a personal unburdening of sin, but also a renewed experience of divine guidance in the daily routine of present-day life.

Confession is like the erasing of a poorly recorded tape, or, as said in psychological technology, the removing of incorrect programming in the brain. In order to erase a tape, the undesirable part of that tape must be wound back to the beginning. Confession is a process of rewinding, going back to the beginning and starting over again. Or, to use other comparisons, the tube in our inner receptor is replaced for the proper reception of the "eternal wave." By confession, we remove interference in our "radar instrument" for receiving God's orders and direction. (*See Appendix IV*).

Isolated Sex and Man's Relation With God

Regarding family planning, the most important question for the Church is: What is the effect of contraceptively isolated sex on man's relationship with God? Are there any kinds of criteria for evaluating the spiritual consequences of this isolation? Can this question be answered by scientists who regard man's spiritual life as a pious emotion rather than an actual reality?

Whatever bases we have for a judgment, they are, above all, the experiences and ideas of people from all religions who have genuine faith in God. In their reports we recognize definite clues as to what is right in the relationship of sexuality to the spiritual life. Regarding the specific relation of contraception to the spiritual life, the Bible is only indirectly helpful, because contraception in its present form was unknown in Biblical times. Thus, we should not expect a definite statement about it in the Bible. But general outlines of a judgment on the matter are present in Scripture and in the spiritual witness of other sources also. In the light of these general clues, people today ought to seriously ask themselves how contraception has affected their relation with God.

When the Anglican Church approved contraceptives in 1930, in its Lambeth Conference, and most of the Lutheran Churches followed that example, the rift widened between these Churches and the Catholic Church, which, except for some confused Catholic thinking in our times, has always regarded contraception as sinful. Sin is whatever separates from God. But how are we to know whether we are separated from God or united with Him?

Dr. Frank Buchman, the founder of the Moral Rearmament Movement, said: "If man listens, God speaks; if man obeys, God acts; and when God acts, miracles occur and people and nations are renewed." [27] In order to be able to listen, I must be completely honest. "Everyone who is of the truth hears my voice" (John 18:37). In order to "see" God's reality I need a pure heart. "Blessed are the pure of heart, for they shall see God" (Matthew 5:8). Purity is protected or restored by confessing, hating and avoiding sin, and making restitution for it.

We can know whether or not our contact with God is real when we are actually concerned about God's will in our lives. Thousands have discovered that absolute purity of heart must be the standard for sexual community in marriage if our contact with God and our experience of His plan are to remain strong. Numerous professors like Kueng, Pfuertner, Auer, Boeckle, the Catholic moral theologians and the Lutheran theologians who recommend the "pill" ought to do a follow-up study. They should investigate the spiritual results of contraception to determine whether Christians who use it are becoming more perceptive of God's will or whether they are losing actual contact with God and are, finally, led by their theologians rather than by God.

An honest evaluation of the spiritual effects of the "pill" requires a radical testing of our own inner attitudes as marriage partners. Husbands must ask themselves whether their wives take "anti-baby pills" because they expect them to do so. Do they feel a sense of responsibility for the bodily and mental health of their wife? We must determine with honesty whether alleged psychological, social and scientific arguments for contraceptives are self-deceptions. Are we, or are we not, prepared to place our creative powers, our longing for pleasure and our self-endorsement within the guidance of the God in whom we profess to believe? We must ask ourselves whether we are willing to permit our strongest energies to be transformed in order to receive God's

guidance in our lives. Is our talk about God and the Church perhaps only rubbish, especially if we do not give God a place in our
strongest desires and urges? Why is it so difficult to forgo sex, even
for a few days, when temperature and ovulation methods of family
planning are just as certain (or uncertain) as the "anti-baby pill"?

We must consider, further, whether the current religious, cultural and political regressions observable everywhere are not the
result of a growing inability to sacrifice sexual passion. We must
wonder what will become of our people if our official public and
private standard is the isolation of sexual pleasure from our creative
mission, from love and community, and if, because of it, the sense
of God's will is destroyed and confusion is permitted to reign. We
must ask ourselves further: Is it Christian for us to conclude from
the biological, psychological, political, economic and theological
arguments put forward for contraception that the human being is
incapable of placing his sexual energies and urges within the control of a higher order?

Indeed, we ought to be clear as to why we do not *wish* to
believe it possible for man to change his sexual behavior. Clearly,
a church that allows the conquest of one evil through another
because it does not believe human beings capable of change has
become hypocritical, dishonest and extremely superfluous.

"The credibility of the Christian message depends in great
measure on the position taken by responsible parents on methods
used to regulate conception," declared twenty Catholic moral
theologians of the Federal Republic of Germany on April 27, 1974.
That is certainly true! But true in exactly the opposite way of those
moral theologians who make the use of the "pill" optional or a
matter of "conscience," without having examined its spiritual
consequences.

An apostolically oriented world congress of lay persons or
a synod that fights for the capitulation of the Church on sexual
morality is not a demonstration of the power of God, but of the
golden calf. The "noble" capitulation speeches made at the Catholics' Day in Essen, where the slogan, "Obey and beget children"
was used with tongue in cheek, verbally erected an altar to Baal.
Neither God nor man was honored there.

Religious Infantilism

A kind of religious infantilism appeared in certain ecclesiastical boards or groups of theology professors who reacted emotionally and unreasonably against *Humanae Vitae*. What ought one to think about Nobel prize winners who obviously are of the opinion that the Pope or the Council could change the standards of honesty, purity, selflessness and love, the eternal foundations of all relationships between God and man and between man and his fellow man? An authentic Pope can try to call attention to these eternal directives, but he certainly cannot change them! When the pearl of God's Kingdom is sold for a pill, how can a Pope bless the sale?

Let it be emphasized here that we are not favoring a Christian theology which is at enmity with the human body, but rather that we are concerned with a very general human experience. We are concerned about the isolation of sexual pleasure from our creative task, the elimination of the Creator Himself from our relationship, and the consequent separation of ourselves from Him. We are also concerned about the age-old evidence that our self-assertion against God is strongest precisely when our will is hardest. Self-will is not the Way of openness to God's will. "Take up your cross and follow me" is a reference to the self-will that needs to be broken.

Transformation of Creative Energy

It is an ancient opinion of inspired men of all religions that sexual power is not only the source of new individual life, but that it can also generate new spiritual life through voluntary abstinence. Such is the experience of successful missionaries and great apostolic workers. We read in the Old Testament that a pure man has the power of ten strong men. St. John and St. Paul willingly refrained from all genital relationships for the sake of their important life work. In ancient cultures, virginity was important for prophecy and inspiration. St. Francis of Assisi, St. Ignatius of Loyola, the great Catherine of Siena, Mahatma Gandhi, and many others influenced both their own times and posterity by sacrificing sex to accomplish their creative work.

The well-known story of the Hittite leader Uriah demonstrates how ancient was the idea of transformation through abstinence. When his master, King David, called him home from besieging a city in order to cover up his (David's) adultery with Bathsheba, Uriah resisted an order from the king to break his promise of abstinence made for the duration of military duty. Although King David had made him drunk, Uriah did not go home to his wife, Bathsheba, but slept on the steps of his house instead. Thus, Uriah unwittingly spoiled the perfidious plans of King David, namely, that Uriah be considered the father of the child Bathsheba had conceived by King David.

Nicholas of Fluee saved Switzerland from a war and became its founder after he, with the consent of his wife Dorothy, was ready to follow the harder path of personal renunciation.

Peter Howard repeatedly emphasized that absolute purity is the spring-board for constructive political concepts and actions according to God's plan.[44] Giving one's energies for the welfare of others instead of wasting them on sexual pleasures or exploitations is one of the great positive possibilities open to us today. Only those men and women who are ready to forgo sex, for shorter or longer periods of time, in order to foster greater tasks and responsibilities for love of God and man have any real credibility and authority in our time. They are the only ones who can give the needed answer to the great world problem of human sexuality.

Contraception and the Sacramental Character of Marriage

Permit me, a Lutheran doctor, to say something about the sacramental character of marriage, because this Catholic idea always has interested me.

If I understand the sacrament correctly, I really cannot understand how Catholic theologians, and even bishops, can regard the isolation of sexual pleasure in marriage, at least in particular cases, as right, while upholding, at the same time, the sacramental character of marriage. Perhaps my meaning will become clear if I explain it in connection with the two other urges for the preservation of life which also are raised to a sacramental level. Just as sexuality serves the preservation of the race, so hunger and thirst serve the preservation of individual life. In human beings they have the same triple purpose as sexuality:

1. the preservation of life;
2. the formation of community;
3. the giving of joy and pleasure.

In the Eucharist these drives are raised to a sacramental level, that is, to a level where man meets and is united with God.

We know that eating and drinking become a disease when they are separated from their original, fundamental meaning of serving the preservation of biological life, and when they are used, instead, to serve only pleasure and the questionable formation of community by drunks and gluttons. Modern medications for over-indulgence witness to the disorder. The isolation of pleasure from the total meaning of any urge leads to disease — which destroys the organism instead of preserving it — and completely abolishes the sacramental character of that drive (1 Cor. 11:27-29).

The full sacramental character of marriage in the Catholic Church, as the meeting place for two persons with God and as the sacred source of human life, needs to be guarded carefully. It is simplistic to expect the teaching ministry of the Church to change an order considered valid for almost two thousand years in order to accommodate highly sophisticated modern contraceptives.

Pope Paul VI and the Opposition

Nevertheless, the opposition against the encyclical *Humanae Vitae* has resembled a revolt. In this age of psycho-sociological sophistication and sexual "freedom," many ecclesiastical critics are afraid of being considered old-fashioned or of getting themselves into a moralistic ghetto. Many Catholic scientists and professors have similar fears. Only a few dare to defend the Pope openly. Some try to pass over the problem in eloquent silence, possibly thinking to themselves: "No pope lives forever; let's wait for the decision of the next one!" But Professor Hans Kueng of Tuebingen did not let the opportunity pass in silence. His attack against the encyclical was loud and vehement.[45]

In the entire discussion following *Humanae Vitae*, I have not once found a critic interested in the innermost concerns of the Pope. Nor have I found "Christian" scientists raising any question as to the effect of sexuality-isolation on the personal relationship of Christians with Jesus Christ. The unbiased observer logically must conclude that this problem, which ultimately is a very serious one for the Church, has no real significance for most critics within the Church. One must wonder about the quality of Christian faith in these critics.

Faith and Science Are Complementary

In our hyper-scientific world today, we need to recognize two valid modes of acquiring knowledge. One mode is an objective-scientific analysis of the external phenomenon of the world. The other is a subjective-intuitive comprehension of the inner reality of the world. The latter precedes the former in actual knowing. Consequently, the Church's teaching never rests primarily on scientific, analytical research, but rather on revealed truth regarding the inner relationship between God and man. This form of knowledge is the basic source of all fundamental pronouncements of the Church.

As two different modes of knowing, faith and science begin and move in different ways. Faith begins to know from within, and then goes outward; that is, it attempts to understand and to evaluate the world from its inner absolute being. Scientific knowledge, on the other hand, begins to know from without and then moves inward. Just as a hollow ball looks different from the outside than from the inside, so the observations of natural science from the outside and religious meditation from the inmost center of being in no way can reach identical conclusions. Yet these are complementary ways of knowing.

Even in science, the dual appearances of matter as wave and particle seem incompatible. Ever-present waves and infinitely small bodies seem to exclude each other logically. Nevertheless, the scientist who is not willing to grasp *both* discoveries, as parts of a complementary whole, no longer works according to sound scientific research.

The Church and the Pope present the truths of revelation. For that reason, scientific arguments within an encyclical are not of primary importance. Whoever expected *Humanae Vitae* to place first priority on analytic science failed to understand the difference between the two modes of knowing. Since an encyclical is not a scientific document, the Pope used in it no scientifically safe, unassailable explanations. Rather, his explanation of the innermost essence of the question, according to his conviction, came from a divine source of knowledge. This source cannot be proven "analytically," but is experientially intuited by one who is united with the reality of God.

A child does not mistrust his own spontaneous knowledge. But if that same child finds himself dishonest in small and large things, he tends to lose faith in his own power to know reality intuitively. Pride, dishonesty and impurity cause intellectual blindness and deafness. The defective result is total dependence on relative scientific knowledge, which starts from external phenomena. Thus, in countries where lies, pretense and official theft of private property are ideologically established, trust in the subjective and intuitive mode of knowing has practically disappeared. This is only logical. In these intellectually deprived countries, like our own, one seeks refuge in the relativity of scientific views, which can be used and manipulated according to need. The human being who no longer has the courage to be a self-appraising, believing, hoping and loving subject then becomes a defenseless object of ideological and technical manipulation.

The "Lesser Evil" Is Still an Evil

Circumstances for a medical doctor constantly force him to choose between two evils, one of which is the lesser evil. Most medications and operations are lesser evils. Similarly, in instances where the sexual control required for natural family planning is lacking, contraception might be regarded as a lesser evil. But now, with the available natural methods being as "certain" or as "uncertain" as the "anti-baby pill," there is no longer any reason for faithful Christians to use the psychologically and medically problematic "pills" or to get injections or to have IUDs inserted into the uterus.[46] (In the United States 20,000 X-ray examinations were made in 1973 because these IUDs had moved into one of the oviducts.)

In cases when the doctor is concerned about the uncontrollable aggression of an alcoholic or over-sexed husband, the use of the "pill" is still a danger. In such a case, as in an operation, it is the lesser of two evils. Often, in spite of the best good will, and because of our own imperfection, we do not succeed in improving the marriage; the attitudes of both partners remain unchanged.

Surely, as individuals, we cannot ignore the sins of our entire society in its materialism and in its creation of a public and private sex craze. We are all part of that society. In some way, we are all at fault for a situation that seems constantly to become more impossible to control. Sometimes we react in self-defense, at first seeing no other way out of a problem than to counsel the lesser of two evils. This "lesser" evil, however, is still an evil. Contraception expresses a lack of desire to subordinate sexual energies to the will and plan of God. As doctors, we are at fault, too, because so often we cannot or do not wish to take the time to help a married couple change their circumstances.

In the United States this problem has been eased by the founding of a "Couple-to-Couple League." Well-informed and convinced married couples instruct other couples in natural family planning methods.

Abandonment of the Person and Society to the "Pill"

If we doctors believe it is totally impossible for our patients to control their sexual urges so that they might decide to forgo sex temporarily, we abandon them to the status of animals or something even worse. We prostitute them spiritually and morally.

Each time a doctor writes a prescription for "pills" because of a lack of time or because of weariness, he simultaneously agrees that the sexual urges cannot be controlled through the use of reason and will, and that his patient has the right to vegetate. Because there are many persons who have solved the problem of family planning correctly, in their own lives and families, the doctor should know that self-control *is* possible.

In the condition of our sexually deteriorated society, however, we certainly are not concerned any longer with the "special case" and the "lesser of two evils." The situation has gotten so far out of hand that people are agitating for free, government-paid "anti-baby pills." At the same time, the negative effects of the "pill" are being systematically suppressed or denied. In the last analysis, we are witnessing an attempt to change, according to the wishes of a liberal consumer-orientated ideology, the standards of right and wrong, as well as the guiding image for man and society.

The old desire for irresponsible "undangerous" sexual relations surely was unleashed by chemical prevention of ovulation. In the frenzy of this new possibility, Church and state were overrun by those hungry for sexual pleasure. An initial concern for allowing the "lesser evil" soon exploded into the "good fortune" of possessing sex as a desired consumer article.

The last obstacle to "the right to unlimited sexual pleasure" is the teaching of the Catholic Church. Other churches already have accepted the current aberrations and have adjusted themselves accordingly.

Rajmohan Gandhi's View; The Pope Is Not Alone

The grandson of Mahatma Gandhi, Rajmohan Gandhi, the chief editor and publisher of the Indian weekly *Himmat*, said that the two Europeans who displayed the greatest courage in 1968 were Pope Paul VI and Germany's Dubcek. "A radical change is necessary in West Germany!" he said. "Do the Germans think primarily only of their comfort, pleasure and security? Will they be satisfied to achieve the greatest perfection in materialism, or will they do everything possible to become a nation of selfless men and women?" Should a leading figure from India understand Pope Paul VI better than a large number of Catholic professors and intellectuals?

One might ask Catholic "pill-Protestants," who no longer heed any religious argument: What would happen to the "infallibility" of the "pill" if, in the next fifty years, the end result were a world-wide counter-catastrophe? Many specialists expect this catastrophe in the third and fourth generation following the beginning of chemical contraception. It was found in animal research that the prevention of ovulation causes chromosomal breaks in the egg cells. These lead to "recessive" hereditary mutilation, which cannot materialize in the first generation, but which is phenomenally typical in succeeding generations when two partners, mutilated in this way, unite.

The same critics who would like to force the Pope to recognize chemical contraception in our time would, then, accuse him most sharply of neglect and irresponsibility. In this way, Catholic professor Mrs. Rank-Heinemann scolded Pope Paul, saying he was to blame for abortion because he did not permit women to use the "pill," thus forcing them to resort to abortion.[47] Those who would have to bear the burden of raising a child with serious hereditary harm would react similarly, but with a much better reason.

A defense of Pope Paul VI and *Humanae Vitae* would be accepted more readily from a Lutheran or a Hindu, who has no religious interest in defending the Pope, than from a Catholic. For this reason Gandhi's view in *Himmat* ought to be exposed further. Among other things he says: "A tidal wave of chastity is possible! Suppression of sexuality is no more a cure than permitting passion to take its course. Chastity is possible and normal. Chastity makes a man or woman interesting, attractive, healthy, intelligent and useful to others. Self-control is not sufficient for purity, but I do not understand why one would discourage those who do not believe in God but who nevertheless wish to lead a disciplined life from trying it. God has an all-inclusive answer for impurity and can purify a person and help him stay pure. If God can deal with the inordinate desires of some of us, he can do the same with the desires of millions of others. A tidal wave of chastity is possible."[23]

I do not agree with everything Gandhi said and demanded, but I do agree with him entirely in his concern about the dangers of an all-out campaign for contraception and sterilization. I also agree with his conviction that a man and woman can live together and love each other without necessarily sleeping together anytime they feel like it. Gandhi continues, "We must be certain not to produce animalized or mechanized human beings for the future. If electric light, transistor radio and television can reach millions, can not chastity do so, too? Like electricity, chastity can come into every home. That would be the next most sensational point of progress for humanity." [23]

Many men and women in the world have discovered the joy and satisfaction of chastity. Now we must make the same experience possible for millions of others. An expansive movement for chastity would accomplish the following:

1. It would control the population explosion in a natural way.
2. It would demand love of human beings for each other, within and outside of the family.
3. It would prepare men and women for creative action and dispose them to work harder to eliminate hunger and misery.

Summary — A Path to Atheism in the Church

Where the chemical and mechanical isolation of sexual pleasure from human sexuality has been in progress for a long period of time, one can see what abuses have resulted. In England, the Anglican Church accepted contraception as early as 1930. This development led to a well-known sexualization of the young generation and to a catastrophic disappearance of faith in that country. The same is true for most of the Lutheran Churches which supported this movement in the past 25 years. The statement of the EKD about sexuality, referred to before, is characteristic.[34] Already it has been the cause of other similar statements.[48]

There is an inner, inexorable logic that works itself out from acceptance of contraception. Once sexual pleasure becomes acceptable in isolation from its procreative function, the next idea to emerge is that every type of sexual pleasure is equally acceptable. This results in a legal "reform" of the sexual penal law, which, in turn, eliminates the ideas of right and wrong from the legal realm of sexual behavior. Finally, we notice a theological surrender of the notions of right and wrong, obedience and sin, in human sexuality. Thus, the idea of sin as "separation" from God does not appear even once in the entire EKD statement.[34] Wherever no standard for good and evil exists, no recognition of sin exists either. Thus, the possibility of purifying our relationship with God and neighbor is likewise dropped.

Finally, if there is no process of regeneration, the loss of sensitivity to God's voice and order leads to a kind of atheism in the Church. A theology of the "death of God" is developed and proclaimed. When divine inspiration no longer is received, man is ruled by negative inspiration. When the body no longer is the "temple of the Holy Spirit," it quickly becomes the "habitation of evil spirits."

Infallible Statements or Infallible Guides?

According to Hans Kueng, there are no absolutely infallible statements in matters of doctrine and morals because these can have different meanings in different contexts.[45] Of course, statements do have different meanings, inasmuch as they are an expression of a definite time-bound "philosophy."

However, the pivotal questions of man's relation to man, formulated in doctrines and morals, are not altered by time-bound views. Certain truths remain essentially unchanged even when they must be explained in terms of the times. For example, the law of gravity never lost its value in spite of basic changes in physics. Although the formal definition of this law has been different at various times, its practical validity remains unchanged even by new perspectives in physics. Relationships between God and man also can be expressed more exactly and clearly by changing the way of saying things. However, "natural laws" and their norms are never basically altered.

The Church's teaching office has the role of instructing men in principles of law and of clarifying these principles as time goes on. If statements of physical science need clarification, so do faith statements. In neither case does clarification of statements mean a change in the reality which the statement is about. Thus, the ideas "descended into hell" and "ascended into heaven" formerly used in the Church's creed are expressed differently today, but the truth of the matter remains unchanged. No one is disturbed by the change in expression; rather, everyone understands the deeper meaning involved. The figurative use of words may be changed to another kind of usage, while people understand that this is not a change in the substance of reality.

The essential part of an "infallible" statement, therefore, is not necessarily its linguistic meaning. Rather, in matters of the Church's doctrine and morals, it is important that a statement express the unchanging essence and eternal order of God's relationship with man. And this need not be done in one everlasting set of words. Statements may be reformulated while expressing the same unchanging essence in a more adequate manner.

The Limitations of Logic

One central problem with formulating truths of faith is the limitation of logic. Some of these truths seem logically impossible. But why should we expect the logic of a three-dimensional world to be adequate for explaining a world of many more dimensions? [49] An example of a seemingly contradictory truth, impossible to three-dimensional logic, is the teaching on predestination and free will. How can we be both predestined and free? (Phil. 2:12).

Modern physics freed us from the domination of a purely three-dimensional perception.[50] It showed us that our logic does not suffice for the understanding of reality. It has shown us that our perception of the objective essence of matter depends upon our subjective choice of a method and instrument of observation. Thus, the apparently contradictory wave and particle appearances of matter result from different methods of observation. One method reveals tiny particles; another method reveals a wave which has a length of 600,000 kilometers and which is, so to speak, omnipresent. The question as to whether a third form of appearance exists is now under consideration.[51] It seems certain that the elementary particle does act in three ways: upon electromagnetic fields as a wave, upon other bodies as a particle, and, in the electronic activity of the human brain, it responds to spirit and will. Therefore, a third qualitative appearance of material energy must exist.

To understand this basic triple character of all material existence is just as impossible with ordinary logic as it is to grasp the Trinity of God, in whose image and likeness man was created, and apparently, also, all other creatures. The logic of a three-dimensional world cannot explain spiritual experience.[51]

Thus, man united with God (Phil. 2:12) will say, in the face of a decision regarding his future destiny, "I must work out my salvation with fear and trembling and make every effort." In retrospect he will say later, "God has wonderfully led me and given me the will, energy and success." These opposing attitudes express the same reality, and both are true. No either/or is possible here!

The post-scholastic emphasis on logic was one of the reasons for the Protestant rift in the Church.[49] Too much human logic began to polarize understanding of truth, so that Luther emphasized one pole, and Church officials the other. Finally, Luther was excommunicated and put under an imperial ban for not accepting the "infallibility" of the Council of Constance.

Confusion resulted regarding faith versus works, Bible versus tradition, nature versus grace, "This is" versus "This symbolizes" in the teaching of the Eucharist, all-embracing Catholicism versus individualistic Lutheranism, unity versus conscience, free will versus predestination. These are not either/or categories, but paradoxical and complementary sides of one truth.

The paradoxical nature of Christian faith in no way implies that "true" or "infallible" statements cannot be made. Because the whole truth cannot be contained in one statement does not mean that statements cannot be "true" or "infallible." Just as the past knowledge of Kepler, Newton, Helmholtz, etc., has not become untrue, but simply has been enlarged upon, other forms of knowledge are expanded. Our task in the Church today is to accept the limitations of logical either/or thinking, to remove the resulting polarizations, and to accept complementary truth and unity as we progress together.

The True Meaning of Infallibility

Today we understand man as a being in a dynamic process of development "on the way" to his final destiny. Thus, we are concerned not so much about formulating exhaustive laws as we are about developing authentic guidelines. Because of the divine importance of our destiny, we need doctrinal and moral guidelines which are "infallible" and lead us unfailingly to our goal. We know such "infallible" guidelines exist because Jesus Himself said: "I am the way, the truth, and the life."

Though His disciples had many false notions, Jesus did not try to change them by discussions or by dogmatic revelations. When He asked His disciples, "Who do people say the Son of Man is?" and "And you, who do you say that I am?" Peter confessed, "You are the Messiah, the Son of the living God!" Christ responded, "No mere man has revealed this to you (no theology professor), but my heavenly Father!" Then He told His disciples they should tell no one that He is Jesus, the Christ (Mt 16:13-17, 20). Why not? Perhaps because the time was not yet right, or because the disciples were not supposed to convince others by teaching the *dogma* of the Sonship of God. This was a truth to be experienced "on the way" with Christ, and which only the Father in heaven reveals to the individual soul.

Today, too, we know that Christian faith exists and flourishes only where it is experienced "on the way." Faith is not learned through theological theories alone. Collapse and crisis exist in the Churches today, in large part, because of a doctrinal rather than an experiential approach to the truth of Christ. Both approaches are necessary. But faith in Christ is first.

Thus we need the "Comforter," the "Spirit of Truth, who leads us on the way of truth." The directive from the Spirit's inner truth and purity will ultimately lead to theological truth. "He who is of the truth, hears my voice." Many millions have experienced that we have "infallible" directives in this sense — not only through the teaching office of the Church, the Pope or a Council — and real Christians need no discussion about it.

The Problem Is Not Infallibility, But Power Politics

For the faithful Lutheran, it is not so much the idea of "infallibility" that is difficult to accept, but rather the misuse of ecclesiastical power. This abuse of power always has been a source of mistrust both in Lutherans and Catholics. However, the religious and moral pacifism that follows a reaction against power politics is just as dangerous as abuse of power. This pacifism assumes that "dialogue and counseling" are able to accomplish everything, and that education alone is able to cast out the devil. Power cannot be saved from degeneration by complete powerlessness.

In Matthew's Gospel, we find that Peter was placed in a position of power, but was tempted to use it in a political way. When Jesus asked, "Who do people say the Son of Man is?" Peter answered "infallibly," "You are the Messiah, the Son of the living God." But because of his wrong judgment regarding the political aspect of the community, Jesus called Peter "Satan."

After Jesus mentioned that the high priests and Pharisees would have Him killed, Peter, wishing to exercise his "office as representative" in order to avoid a catastrophe, immediately interrupted Jesus, chiding Him, "May that not happen to you." Naturally, he would try to urge Jesus to avoid a confrontation with political and religious leaders in order to avoid his tragic crucifixion. Peter apparently tried to persuade Jesus to accept co-existence with the mighty ones, or a weakening in the essence of the Kingdom of God.

If Jesus had presented the notion of the Messiah as a great world ruler, who would conquer the Romans by means of a bloody revolution and rule the people with an iron hand, He would not have been in conflict with the priests, Pharisees and Zealots. If He had exhorted them to hate their enemies, which was necessary in the opinion of the Jewish leaders, His preaching would have been more acceptable. However, Jesus rejected the idea of God's Kingdom coming through a revolutionary change of social conditions. He said to Pilate: "Yes, I am a king. For this I was born. For this I came into the world: to be a witness to the truth. My Kingdom is not of this world. If it were of this world, my servants would come and fight for me. But it is not of this world" (John 18:36).

Instead of teaching the ways of political power, Jesus said: "Love your enemies. . . . Change your hearts. . . . First remove the beam from your own eye before you remove the splinter from your brother's eye." The way to change the world is by regeneration, "rebirth." The Kingdom of God begins in the inner personality and not in outer political change. Therefore, evolution, not revolution, is the way of the Kingdom. Not poisoning by hatred but strengthening by charity cures the sick. Not a crusade, but the bearing of one's cross is the way of the Messiah.

In the Old Testament, there are many different concepts of the Kingdom of God and the Messiah. Since Jesus appeared precisely at the moment when the Jews suffered most from the colonial imperialism of the Romans and longed for power in their weakness, the Jewish people had to decide what was meant by the Kingdom of God. Was this Kingdom a new social order or a new inner life? The choice had to be made between Barabbas and Jesus. They chose Barabbas and crucified Jesus.

The choice is still being made today. We still have representatives of the theology of revolt in the Churches (the Zealots and Iscariots) who crucify Christ anew. And we still have those, on the other hand, who believe the Kingdom of God will come through hearing and obeying and bearing the cross.[27]

When, in the chair of Peter, the pursuit of power politics was greater than the search for the Kingdom of God, Christianity was divided into "Greek-Orthodox," "Roman-Catholic" and "Germanic-Protestant" groups. After that, the term "Catholicism" was not an expression of an all-embracing unity, but of a division in Christianity. In this divisive situation, "humanly" speaking, there are only two "political-tactical" possibilities for us. Either we must "Let fire drop from heaven and annihilate them" (the way of active force), or we must accommodate ourselves by co-existing and lessening our claims to having the absolute truth. Only these two ways, bloody revolution or co-existence for "pastoral reasons" could bypass the third way, the cross. In the light of the cross, we remember Christ's words: "If they persecuted me, they will also persecute you."

In the end, co-existence might not be possible. The attack now being made against Christian rights and the Christian image of man in formerly Christian nations is so demoniacal that Rome must wonder what will happen to the Church if the red revolution is permitted to obliterate the West. Where can the Church look for help? In time, will the Church be pressed to leave the sinking ship in order not to sink with it? Is not its Master's order, "Depart from her, my people, for fear of sinning with her (the whore of Babylon) and sharing the plagues inflicted on her" (Apoc. 18:4) meaningful for the Church today?

Co-existence is infectious and makes us cooperators in guilt. Will we co-exist with the "beast from the depth," the "false prophet" of Marxism and the "red dragon" of Maoism, which hate and destroy the "Atlantic whore" on account of her riches and degeneracy (Apoc. 12:13)? The alternative is patience and the "faith of saints," the rule of God in our personal lives, and the way of the cross.

There is a constant danger, however, that "Peter" would say, "Spare yourself," or "May that not happen to you!" "Peter" might want to avoid complete confrontation with the "beast from the depth." Who would not understand Peter and Pope Paul VI completely if, as "representatives" and shepherds, they tried to give their sheep a little breathing space by protecting them from the cross and physical annihilation? What great suffering and struggle would prompt the Pope "to abandon ship" and walk on the water of Eastern politics, which heretofore sustained no one? The waves of these waters might engulf him, so that his only hope would be the Master's saving hand.

However, we know that the wrong political course which Peter wanted to force upon Christ — and the severe reprimand which he received for it — did not lead to Peter's removal from the office of successor of Christ. Nor did it affect his knowledge of doctrine and morals. In our own day, divisive mistrust of Rome is due more to its past and present power politics than to statements on faith and morals.

The point is that power politics, and even an immoral life in popes, does not necessarily affect their ability to teach infallible guides. It seems senseless to quarrel about this matter. Even a pope like Alexander VI, who was not a "temple of the Holy Spirit" in his daily life, but much more a "house of the impure spirits," could be guided exclusively by the Holy Spirit in questions of doctrine and morals. We agree that popes and council members ought to be "temples of the Holy Spirit," not only because of their office, but in their personal lives as well. But there was a Judas among the twelve apostles. So there are popes and ecclesiastical leaders who can be led by the Spirit of Darkness. Indeed, the coming of false "Christs" and prophets, who will lead many astray, is predicted. Christ Himself warns us to be cautious and mistrustful, so as not to fail to notice the works of the powers of darkness.

By Their Fruits You Will Know Them

There is no better test for the office of Peter than that its occupant proves to be a *petros*, a rock upon whom all Christians can depend, so that the Church will not be overcome by the gates of hell.

Contrary to Dr. Kueng and his friends, many Lutherans, among them many doctors, thanked Pope Paul for *Humanae Vitae*. Indeed, many were relieved. They had feared that the last moral bulwark and spiritual authority remaining in the modern world which had not yet capitulated to the golden calf might fall down on its knees before Baal and worship the spirit of the sexual revolution. Considering the unusual pressure to do so, both from within and outside the Church, these fears were highly warranted.

In view of the harmfulness of contraception to the spiritual life of union with God, as explained elsewhere in this book, the Church would mislead millions by proclaiming such an evil acceptable. Probably no other papal decision in history has helped so much to cancel the old mistrust against the papacy. When Pope Paul remained steadfast against pressure from the entire world, when he chose the cross instead of an easier way, the credibility of the papacy was restored.

Countless faithful Protestants were grateful for the teaching office of the Catholic Church, as well as for the Pope. This shows us that the way to unity is not to discard the teaching office of the Church, but to purify its bearer by penance and the forgiveness of sins committed in the name of this office and the Church.

The attack by Professor Kueng and his friends against Pope

Paul VI was not evolutionary, as they supposed, but counter-evolutionary. The "freedom of conscience" which they have promoted for the sake of "pill-Protestants" already has become "freedom of conscience" for abortion.[41] Already, the Catholic theologian Professor Greinacher and many Lutheran professors, like Moltmann of Tuebingen and Dantine of Vienna, etc., defend abortion at any time during pregnancy.[41] And they do so on medical, legal and theological grounds.

Those who promote "freedom" for abortion seem indifferent to the fact that abortion upon request will lead to ten times more abortions. They seem unconcerned that the spiritual-moral foundation of the medical profession will be destroyed as medical credibility is sacrificed for the purpose of socialistic killing. Apparently, it does not matter to the "freedom" theologians that 30% of aborting women will be harmed permanently, and that violence will be encouraged in our affluent society. Indeed, their consciences are not even touched when they see public knowledge of right and wrong reversed. They ignore the fact that millions are losing their understanding of guilt and sin, and that the course of numerous women, men and doctors is ending in revolt against God. In the face of this surprising "tolerance," the sincere lay person asks himself what else these theologians will say to their communities and to the world.

Professor Kueng's colleagues, Professor Pfuertner and Mr. Ell, spell out the logical conclusion of contraception by advocating premarital sex, and Mr. Ell calls this new "progressive" approach "dynamic sexual morality."

When acts previously considered immoral are now accepted in terms of "dynamic sexual morality," it is not surprising that some professors abolish the whole idea of sin and end up attacking the existence of the devil. If Martin Luther were to hear these professors, he well might again throw that famous ink-well with which he is supposed to have chased the devil in *Wartburg*. The Lutheran Christian of today might ask whether the de-sacramentalizing of marriage was a mistake. To be sure, Martin Luther's "leitmotif" was not freedom from the commandments of God and sexual morality, but the freedom of the Christian for his real destiny: being God's "partner" in the plan of creation.

"Infallible" Professors

While Professor Kueng and his friends are of the opinion that Pope Paul VI "harmed the Church incalculably" with his encyclical, others are convinced that, because of the encyclical, the Pope saved the Church and other parts of Christianity from inner decay.[45] He was prompted by a true, unbending spirit of humility, seeking to obey God rather than men. He experienced the suffering of "not being able to do otherwise" when he decided against contraception in spite of unusual world pressure. In this unyielding adherence to truth, Pope Paul was in harmony with the original battle of the reformers, who were concerned with purity and justice in the Church.

In his attacks against the Pope and *Humanae Vitae*, Hans Kueng never refutes the theses and statements of the encyclical in a clear and direct manner. Instead, he criticizes in generalities, without making biblically founded suggestions. In one of his "infallible" writings, Kueng denies the possibility that Pope Paul should understand the promise given to Peter in terms of personal inspiration.[45] He wishes to prescribe that the Pope may act "only in spiritual community and unbroken solidarity with the whole Church." The "ideal" Pope, Kueng maintains, would never regard the promise made to Peter as a promise to give personal inspiration to the Pope, but only as a special support in the context of the Church, to whom the Spirit is promised as a whole.

It is surprising how Kueng's burning desire to curb the Pope blinds him to the total truth. How often has there been in the Church a situation of "unbroken solidarity and community"? If popes were allowed to work only in such utopian conditions, most would have passed their entire time in office without being able to act at all.

Both Priest and Prophet

Professor Kueng apparently forgets that the papal office is not only a priestly or teaching office but also an apostolic or prophetic one. All of these qualities are part of the office filled by the successor of Peter. These give to the office a maximum of responsibility, especially necessary during times of severe crisis when opposing ideas threaten the unity of the Church. Precisely in such times, as we have today, there is no "spiritual solidarity and community of ultimate responsibility of the whole Church." Therefore, the demands of Professor Kueng are illusory.

In so far as his office is priestly, the Pope represents all before God when he dispenses the sacraments, gives God's blessing, asks forgiveness and prays for the Church. However, he must be equally aware of his office as prophet when, like Moses, he stands alone against all, teaching the commandments and will of God, and casting their golden calf from its throne. What else could the title *petros*, the "rock," mean? The "rock" holds out against all softness, resists storms and floods (including the flood of sex) which threaten the Church. The Pope, as prophet, sees a deeper solidarity and spiritual community between men and the Church, one which comes from the "unbroken solidarity and spiritual community" between the Lord and the Church. Thus, a leader of the Church has opposing duties of being a priest *for all*, and of standing *against all*, as prophet, when necessary.

However, a pope can fulfill this twofold task only if he is not hindered from taking the promise to Peter as a promise for "personal inspiration." Matthew 28:20, as well as Matthew 16:18, is relevant: "And know that I am with you always until the end of the world!" Likewise, the promise of Jesus to send the "Comforter," the "Spirit of truth, who will teach you all truth" (John 16:13; 14:16, 26) is relevant to the office of the Pope.

Why should a really faithful Pope not understand these promises as being favorable to personal inspiration? Why should this promise be taken as favoring inspiration only in a general way, for "the entire Church," and then be left to various theological schools to decide what is meant by it? As a Lutheran Christian, I fail to understand why the Pope should not be personally inspired.

It seems to me that a modern, collectivistic and socialistic heresy is overcoming Professor Kueng. The notion that the "democratic" majority is right is flatly contradicted by reality. The Holy Spirit was promised neither to the "Church" as an indefinable whole, nor to some democratic majority in the Church, but to those who are prepared to be "temples of the Holy Spirit," or those who listen to and obey the Spirit.

This point might be clarified by a comparison. Like electricity, the Holy Spirit "enlightens" not "the whole city," but each individual "house" and "room," *if* the electric bulbs are not burned out and all the conduits are in good order. In the event that the lights no longer shine in the houses of the majority, but only a few lamps flicker, the situation will not be helped by saying that the electric lights of "inspiration" were promised only to the city as a whole. One has to repair the conduits of individual houses and replace burned-out bulbs so that lights can shine for the entire city.

Personal Inspiration: An Alternative in a Conflict

I have the distinct impression that Catholic and Lutheran "pill-Protestants" are, at times, out of touch with the Bible, the Word of God. They seem to lack personal experience of divine inspiration and guidance. Many of us who had to go through the hell of a past war and who experienced how "infallibly" God can lead us might have an advantage. It is clear to us that God's guidance can "infallibly" lead us through all kinds of detours and difficulties, in spite of our failings and stupidities.

The "infallible" way to a common goal and to a final unity of Christians demands personal inspiration not only for the Pope but for every person who desires to reach his goal. Hans Kueng does not seem to recognize this inspiration as providing a third way different from the two sides in a conflict. According to his opinion, the Pope has two possible ways to reach a decision: either he follows the counsel of the majority by recommending the free use of contraception (after giving all manner of scientific, sociological, psychological and political reasons for it), or he follows the minority that upholds the teachings of faith and revelation. In the words of Hans Kueng, "He follows either the progressive majority, which favored contraception, or he follows the conservative minority, which opposed contraception." [45] Since Hans Kueng recognized only these two possible ways, he concludes: "The Pope decided against all the practical arguments of the specialists appointed by himself, in favor of the infallibility of doctrine. And at what costs! Unfortunately, one must say: at the great cost of Church and Pope and their credibility . . ." (page 49, *Unfehlbar*).

Did the Pope Act Without Collegiality?

Professor Kueng complains that the Pope wrote the encyclical in uncollegial aloneness, and that "he neither seriously considered nor refuted the official statements of the commission."

One must ask Professor Kueng where, in this appraisal of the majority of "all those theologians and bishops, doctors, demographers, and other specialists, who worked and discussed for years" is the answer to the question regarding the effect of artificial contraception on the relationship of the faithful with God? This most important question was not touched with even a single word! Since the Pope did not speak as psychologist, sociologist, biologist, doctor or politician, but as the one most responsible for the Church, he could not use the appraisal of the majority, and thus did not refute it.

The Pope and the Christian who choose God's will for primary guidance, rather than just objective scientific arguments, will not be persuaded by a scientifically minded majority. The question as to whether contraception separates man from God and is sinful cannot be decided simply by papal or majority decree. Apparently, the divinely provided norms for man's partnership with God in creation did not meet with the approval of many a psychologist and theologian. Where, then, are the scientists' practical experiments which would prove their assertions that contraception is spiritually and physically harmless?

The twenty German moral theologians who attacked Pope Paul VI and his encyclical on April 27, 1974, would have done better, as paid appointees representing the Church, if they had done the proper research to bring light to this critical question. At the very least, they should have been concerned about the spiritual effects of contraception. Instead, they left the choice of the method to the conscience of the partners, while giving them no standards according to which decisions of conscience could be made. But a decision made without proper standards transforms conscience into an oracle replacing God.

The only standards that interest the twenty theologians seem to be sociological trends. They appear to be concerned about trends emerging in the dialogue between theologians and the human sciences since 1968 on the nature of marriage and sex morality. Has the dialogue with the sciences and social trends become more important to moral theologians than the dialogue with the Scriptures or with God? Or do they think these latter forms of dialogue are impossible? And what are their "objective reasons" for not accepting *Humanae Vitae*? Is God not an objective Lord for the faithful Christian, as well as a source of subjective experience? Must "objective reasons" not be measured against man's subjective and objective relationship with God before seeking counsel from the sciences?

The above position of the German theologians only serves to show that the Pope was forced into solitude — because the pivotal point of the theological problem involved in *Humanae Vitae* was not considered by anyone else! Who but God, the Lord of the Church, could answer this pivotal question? Is it really so difficult to imagine a direct conversation of the Pope with the Lord of the Church, in prayer and fasting, listening and begging, weeping and self-denial? Is it impossible to imagine that the representative of Christ would rather obey God than the "progressive majority" or the "conservative minority?"

Humanae Vitae *and the Question of Infallibility*

Hans Kueng's insistence that the Pope decided in favor of "infallibility" over other valid arguments is false. When *Humanae Vitae* was published, the Pope did not claim infallibility. He knew full well that his decision against the wishes of Cardinals, bishops, scientists, politicians and large segments of the masses would precipitate an unprecedented attack against the dogma of papal "infallibility" in matters of doctrine and morals. Such an attack would have been more dangerous and severe than that against Vatican I, which led to the separation of a small group of Catholics.

On the other hand, there was no danger that papal infallibility in matters of doctrine and morals would be questioned by the rest of the world if the Pope had decided in favor of the "pill." He would have been celebrated everywhere as a great reformer of the Church, indeed, as a religious redeemer of the world. To everyone's joy, he would have seemed to solve the age-old conflict between unrestrained sexual pleasure and divine inspiration, between ecstatic eroticism and genuine religious experience, between Baal and Jehovah. If only the Pope had blessed the free consumption of "anti-baby pills," little or nothing would have been said about infallibility. But Pope Paul VI was clear about the situation and the problem. He knew that an unpopular decision had to be made.

A Decision for the Cross, Not for Infallibility

We must wonder why the Pope ultimately decided in favor of "divine" and "human" arguments instead of "practical" ones, and why he did so in spite of what Kueng calls "great costs to the Church and the Pope and their credibility." Is Professor Kueng so blind as to think the Pope took all this upon himself for the sake of the dogma of his own infallibility? Like his predecessors, Pope Paul never spoke *ex cathedra* on family planning. In connection with this issue, the term "infallibility" never was used officially.

In a talk in July, 1968, Pope Paul gave his reasons for deciding as he did. He explained his great effort to know the will of God in this matter.

> We will say only a few words to you, not on the document itself but on some of the feelings that filled our mind during the rather lengthy period of its preparation.
> The first feeling was that of our own very grave responsibility. It brought us into and sustained us in the heart and core of the question for the four years of study and planning that went into this encyclical. We will confide too that this feeling caused us no small measure of mental anguish. We never felt the weight of our office so much as in this situation. We studied, read and discussed all we could; and we also prayed a great deal.
> You are already aware of some of the circumstances sur-

rounding this matter. We had to give an answer to the Church, to the whole of mankind. We had to evaluate a traditional doctrine that was not only age-old but also recent, having been reiterated by our three immediate predecessors; and we had to do this with all of the sense of obligation and all of the liberty that go with our apostolic duty. We had to make our own the Council's teaching, which we ourself had promulgated. Even though the conclusions of the commission established by Pope John, of venerable memory, and enlarged by us, were only of a consultative nature, still we felt inclined to accept them, insofar as we thought we could; but at the same time we realized we had to act with all due prudence.

We knew of the heated, passionate and authoritative discussion on this very important subject. We heard the loud voices of public opinion and of the press. We listened to the softer voices that penetrated into our paternal, pastoral heart — the voices of many people, especially of highly respected women, who were distressed by this difficult problem and by their own even more difficult experience with it. We read the scientific reports on alarming population problems, often supported by the studies of experts and by government programs. We received publications from all directions, some of them based on a study of particular scientific aspects of the problem, others on a realistic consideration of many grave demands arising from the changes that have burst forth in all areas of modern living.

Many times we felt as if we were being swamped by this wave of documents; and many times, humanly speaking, we felt our own humble inadequacy in the face of the formidable apostolic task of having to speak out on this matter. Many times we trembled before the dilemma of giving in easily to current opinions, or of making a decision that would be hard for modern society to accept, or that might be arbitrarily too burdensome for married life.

We consulted many people with high moral, scientific and pastoral qualifications. We invoked the enlightenment of the Holy Spirit and put our mind at the complete disposal of the voice of truth, striving to interpret the divine law that rises from the intrinsic requirements of genuine human love, from the essential structures of the institution of marriage, from the personal dignity of the spouses, from their mission in the service of life and from the holiness of Christian marriage. We reflected on the enduring elements of the traditional doctrine in force in the Church, and then in particular on the teachings of the recent Council. We pondered the consequences of one decision and the other; and we had no doubts about our duty to set forth our decision in the terms expressed in the present encyclical.

Is **Humanae Vitae** *for Protestants, Too?*

A Lutheran following this entire explanation might begin to wonder about the true meaning of Matthew 16:18, "You are Peter and upon this rock I will build my Church, and the gates of hell shall not prevail against it." Was this promise made not only for Peter, but for his successors as well? Otherwise, how would a Pope, like Paul VI, have enough courage to follow his innermost conviction and inspiration, and decide against the majority? Could he choose this difficult way at all if he did not face the *Quo Vadis?* (Where are you going?) of his Master?

Apparently, Pope Paul VI is more "Lutheran" than many Lutheran and Catholic progressive theologians who believe that all problems can be dissected with the knife of "three-dimensional" logic, and then solved accordingly. The truly "Lutheran" approach emphasizes correct spiritual and religious reality more than logical analysis.

When a pope struggles to make an unusually important decision for the Church and the world, for the sake of God's will; when he prays, suffers, and listens after examining the facts carefully, his decision, as one made through the Holy Spirit, is decisive for Lutherans also. What is taught, then, are guidelines which lead infallibly to the goal. If a pope teaches such guidelines without concern for the demands of power or being right at any price, if he is no longer interested in "Roman politics," if he does not try to master difficulties tactically only, assuring himself of the approval of the "democratic" majority, then I cannot believe that Christ will fail him. He has searched, with all his heart, for a clear answer.

The Encyclical and Inspiration

It is time that Professor Kueng and all those who defend "free use of pills" examine the story of the high priest Aaron and similar stories in the Old and New Testaments. Perhaps then they would better understand why Pope Paul VI hesitated to yield to the majority, thus giving them a more comfortable religion, as did the high priest Aaron, who did not want to lose his influence over the majority. It was precisely the fear of the "majority's" opinion that influenced most of the bishops and theologians who were opposed to *Humanae Vitae.*

Just as the degree of transparency in a crystal rock depends upon its inner structures, so the degree of inspiration in the Pope's message is determined by his inner purity. Simultaneously, he needs other human capabilities and qualities, as well as an education, in order to be qualified for his office. But his inner ability to receive inspiration remains primary in importance.

Certainly, the Master of history and of the Church can "write straight with crooked lines" and prevent an unsuited pope from making wrong decisions, or correct such mistakes through further developments. This would present no problem to the faith of those who are convinced that the Master of history will lead the Church "infallibly" to its goal.

If, in the future, the degree of "infallibility" could be determined not only by the office of the Pope, but also by the bearer's personal transparency for God's word and by his submission to Christ, then the fear of the misuse of papal power would disappear in those who oppose the papacy. Thus, numerous Lutheran Christians and doctors who support Pope Paul VI and *Humanae Vitae* have said that Kueng's attack against "infallibility," at this point in time, was a decided anachronism. Christianity does not need more sexual license or further divisions at this time.

What is urgently needed for our world and the world of tomorrow is a modern ideal of the rule of God. We need a world in which that ideal will be the heart of marriage, family and human sexuality, as Pope Paul VI described it in *Humanae Vitae.* To develop and demonstrate such an ideal as an answer to sexualism, liberalism, Communism, racism, humanism, nationalism and pacifism is a task which could be very rewarding, even for theology professors. I am sure they would offer their Church, their people and their students much more this way than by a revolt in the wrong place at the wrong time.

Host or "Pill"?

The Christian cannot find a single solid reason in the Old and New Testaments, or in Christian tradition, for the isolation of sexual pleasure from its creative or communal task. Self-interest concerns itself with the two partners, their tensions, fears, problems and needs, while it disregards both the child's right to life and God's right to rule. This self-centered view is basically so narrow that it merits little discussion. Thus, self-centered and sentimental commentaries on *Humanae Vitae* have been doomed to failure.

To revolt against the papal decision on sexuality and human life is dangerous for the individual Catholic. There is a definite contradiction involved in taking both the "pill" and the host, both the isolation of sex from its Christian totality, and the Eucharist, at the same time. In principle, the Lutheran, too, cannot serve both God and Baal at once. And, as the position of Rajmohan Gandhi shows, not only a Christian but also a world-wide decision is involved.

The visions of the Seer of Patmos in the last chapters of the New Testament, hidden in deep mystery for centuries, suddenly now become more understandable. Thus the physicist Bernard Philbert, of Munich, tries to explain these visions in his book on Christian prophecy and nuclear energy.[52] Likewise, Dr. Basilea Schlink, foundress of the Lutheran Sisterhood of Mary in Darmstadt, describes the vision of the "Babylonian harlot" in her booklet "Zum erstenmal, seit es Kirche Jesu Christi gibt."[53] The harlot rules peoples who once were Christian but who sold their divine calling for sexual pleasure and luxuries unknown to them before. The harlot becomes the guiding ideal of society. As portrayed in the Book of Revelation, she sits "on all waters," enriching "all kings of the earth" with her sex traffic and making them "drunk with the wine of prostitution."

Besides the harlot, the "beast from the depth" sees that "no one will be able to buy or sell anything unless he has the sign of the beast on his hand and forehead." That is, only he who is prepared to take on the sign of Cain, agreeing in thought and deed with the anti-Christian system, will be able to have any property. There will be "great signs in the heavens." Finally the harlot, Babylon, which will be burned in an hour (possible only through the atom bomb), will be completely annihilated. One third of all human beings will be killed, seas and lakes polluted, and the great final battle over Jerusalem will take place between the Gulf of Aqabah and Armageddon. World events do seem to be conspiring in that direction.

God or Chaos?

"Must we come to a complete destruction of our civilization and a catastrophe of unimaginable proportion, or is a change possible?" asked Dr. Frank Buchman, founder of the group for moral rearmament. Will Leonid Brezhnev's idea, made public in his speech commemorating Lenin's hundredth birthday on April 22, 1970, come true? Brezhnev said,

> Out there in the West we find an enormous wave of crime, the dark winds of narcotics and pornography, and the perversion of emotions and maimed souls. The deterioration of morals in the West will result in the absolute triumph of international Socialism and Communism.

Many already are saying, "Nothing will help us now! Our fate is sealed!" But Buchman sees a possibility for a change of course that can reverse the destructive trends.

It is up to us to choose. Are we prepared to respond to God's word? Will we make efforts today to build a better world for tomorrow? Will we, as images of God, choose the way of authentic freedom, or will we go the way of a reactionary, materialistic destruction of man? Will we choose Christ or the anti-Christ?

One thing is clear. In the end, a completely godless and dehumanized world will not exist. Nor will it be a world of irrational liberalism or racism. All these idols will pass away. We are free to affirm the "Kingdom of God," which can be and must be our personal, cultural, economic, political and religious goal through every catastrophe.

"It is my desire that the world will be ruled by men who permit God to lead them. Why do we not permit God to rule the world?" These were Dr. Frank Buchman's last words, which he spoke haltingly and laboriously to his friends on his deathbed in Freudenstadt in the Black Forest.[54] These words point out the answer to the sexual counter-evolution, and to other social revolts and catastrophes.

"Remain faithful until death and I will give you the crown of life" (Apoc. 2:10), "for I am the Alpha and the Omega, the Beginning and the End," says the Lord, "who is and who was and who is to come, the Almighty" (Apoc. 1:8).

APPENDIX I

Evolution Through "Chance and Necessity," or Through Creation?

In his book *Zufall und Notwendigkeit* (Chance and Necessity) Professor Jacques Monod tries to establish the endless number of possible variations which set in motion the play of chance with genetic patterns. He sees these variations as an exclusive explanation for the higher development of life since the existence of the first cell. But in chance alone, in the pressure of selection, in the struggle for existence and in the surprising stability of genetic patterns once set up, there is no satisfactory explanation about the origin of the powers and tendencies of "building materials" that make it possible for these materials to become a living part of a higher organism.

One can build an endless variety of structures from wood, stone, glass, etc., but the building materials always need the architect's plan and the mason's work. This comparison may seem primitive, and an imperfect parallel. The "building materials" in our bodies — the elementary particles, atoms, molecules and cells — not only have the power of being parts of a higher plan and quality of existence, but they are able to respond both to spiritual orders and to each other. Thus, they can have a spiritual quality. This important quality of the "building materials" is not easily explained by the thesis of "chance and necessity."

This does not mean that chance and the other factors of development, which Monod and others allege, do not play an important role in the process of evolution. The power of "self-organization in the building stones" (to which Professor Manfred Eigen refers in his contribution to the book *Ludus Vitalis*, in order to make a comparison with Hermann Hesse's *Glassbeadgame*) prompts him to say, "God throws dice, but he follows the rules of the game!" One is reminded of a quotation from the biblical story of creation in Genesis 1:24, "And God said, 'Let the earth bring

forth all kinds of living creatures.' " He said, "Let the earth . . .";
this means that *matter* had "inherent," innate power to cooperate
in creation from the beginning.

However, it is an unscientific exaggeration for Professor
Monod to maintain that blind chance is the *only* factor in evolution. It would be equally wrong if one were to reduce the origin
of "information" solely to the origin of definite molecules which
may serve as a reserve in the nucleus or in brain cells.

The fact that Professor Monod and others are not ready to
recognize other reasons for evolution is no proof that these reasons
do not exist. Based on countless new scientific findings, an increased probability exists that new reasons for evolution could be
found. Physical powers and activities are measured with appropriate instruments. Physical-chemical research methods, therefore,
are proper only where physical-chemical appearances are measured. The quality of spiritual impulses, ideas, plans, will-power,
attitudes, etc., cannot be measured with physical-chemical methods (even though these ideas, etc., use physical-chemical carriers
of information), because these spiritual qualities are more than
merely physical-chemical. Reducing reality to physical-chemical
appearances, therefore, is an arbitrary act of faith which is unusually unscientific. Dr. Karl Gunning, president of the Dutch
doctors and of the "World Federation of Doctors Who Respect
Human Life," has shown this clearly. He says that it is high time
we include all of reality, not merely a part of it, in our scientific
thought and research.

In spite of the fact that thoughts and impulses of the will
cannot be measured, it is apparent that the elementary particles —
atoms, molecules, cells and organs of our bodies — respond to the
will and spirit, and carry out their orders. It is also apparent that
a tape is not changed quantitatively when it receives a recording,
but is electromagnetically changed qualitatively so that it can
transmit a new quality. The qualitative power of our elementary
particles is possible only when they possess a third form of appearance. A qualitative form, appropriate to the spiritual form, which
makes responses to the spirit possible, must exist over and above
the electromagnetic quality of a wave or a particle. This is a quality to which the waves or particles can respond. The physicist

Bernhard Philberth explained this type of understanding of living matter, with its three forms of appearances, as a "triune," "trinitarian" dimension in his book *Der Dreieine.*[51]

We experience the power of our physical-chemical energies to respond to spirit and will in the activity of our brains. If these energies are capable of reacting to spirit in the brain, they are, in principle, also capable of doing so in other parts of our organism. Thus the spiritual impulse, aimed at the elementary particles, atoms, molecules, genes and chromosomes of our genetic information, is also possible. Directed, aimed and planned influences on the genetic program are just as conceivable as "accidental" physical-chemical ones. As long as this point is not absolutely disproved, the attempt to limit the possibility of mutations to physical-chemical, quantitative reactions, and to reject the qualitative, spiritual impulses as non-existent, must be regarded as totally unscientific. In the material world around us, we find not only "accidental" changes, but countless desired, planned and directed influences. We know that such changing spiritual influences are not the products of individual brain cells alone, just as we know that pictures and sounds are not the products of television tubes alone. The brain of someone who is hypnotized can be changed qualitatively. These changes (mutations) induce the hypnotized person, after awakening, to perform entirely different actions from those he might have intended. Whoever pays attention to this notices, again and again, a so-called carry-over of thoughts from person to person, especially in persons of the same inner persuasion. The Bible maintains that this is the way God or his messengers guide and direct the person who is prepared to cooperate. Such thoughts and suggestions, given like radio signals, often change the world considerably.

A person no less than Einstein is supposed to have pointed out that intuitive knowledge is the highest form of human knowledge (Professor Jens, Tuebingen). Likewise, many Soviet attempts with para-psychology and countless other efforts elsewhere point to the possibility of influence on, and change of, matter. The attempt to question the creative, spiritual impulse in evolution is, therefore, not only an arbitrary ideological distortion of fact but a solution simply not acceptable today, even though it is clothed in the intellectuality of Monod.

To describe the relationship between evolution and creation, one could compare an exhibition of paleontological fossils of the first living beings to a showing of the development of cars. In the development of a modern Mercedes from the oxcart, one can find small improvements, even as one does in the development of the human species. One can notice the result of competition, improved adjustments to surroundings, consumer tastes, etc. The poorer types disappear and the better models are retained. The process of selection is truly an important one in developing new cars. "Chance" and "necessity" also help. Still, no one would say that the discoverers and engineers responsible for planning and development are imaginary just because they cannot be identified with, and discovered in, the individual types of cars. Neither can one conclude, from the exterior of the car, how changes or improvements in quality (mutations) came to be. One can only surmise this, as one must surmise the evolution of a species and of its various types of behavior.

Since the beginning of modern times, science is increasingly concerned with observing, comparing, describing and judging external appearances. Thus, the "object" is seen and recognized from without, from the surface. Thus "objective" scientific knowledge is always comparative, "relative" and not associated with values. When the observed item or appearance is made the "object" of observation or a "thing," the corresponding scientific observation is "material" and "free from emotion."

However, science, critical of itself, knows that this method is "superficial" and not suited to judge the innermost reality of things or to classify values. It knows that the scientific, analytical, objective and relative understanding of the development of human knowledge is secondary, and that it presupposes the primary intuitive grasp of the inner reality of the world and its appearances. Adam gave all the animals a "name." The Greek word for "name" is *onoma*, which means name and essence, a characteristic sign of inner reality.

At first, a child does not know scientifically or objectively, but subjectively — from within outward. After that, the child learns categories and ideas with names, which make a scientific, abstract, relative and objective understanding from without possible. Subjective understanding of reality is absolute and evaluating. We can change nothing about an inner impression. If Einstein regards the intuitive knowledge of reality as the highest form of human knowledge, this is because intuition can make the reality of things meaningful and because scientific knowledge is not concerned with meanings and values. Indeed, the most ingenious forms of science are not possible without "inspirations," "ideas," "suggestions," "illuminations" and "revelations."

Professor Monod, therefore, makes a basic mistake when he reduces intuition to the "animistic" level and considers only the purely objective form of human knowledge valid. However, he does not notice how subjective he himself suddenly becomes when he minimizes subjective human understanding. His extremely unorthodox use of scientific knowledge becomes clear, also, in the way he uses the idea of "chance."

As long as one cannot understand evolution in its inner being, strictly in a scientific way, then science remains a pure description of outer objective appearance. The inner meaning of "chance" mutation remains unexplained. Of course, if one wishes to explain the idea of "chance" and mutation to mean an "accidental" occurrence (in the sense of the opposite of a meaningful, planned effect determined by a higher goal), then the idea of "chance" is definitely a negative value judgment against creation. Here Monod is guilty of an unscientific exaggeration, since he takes ideas from the realm of belief. If one understands all mutations to mean chance, as an exclusively blind, senseless, goalless running-down of a mechanism, one ideologizes science to the point of materialistic faith. Only that theory which admits all reality, without contradictions, has the right to be called science in the best sense of the word. This form of science seeks to know reality as much from its essence, from within outward, as from its appearance, from without inward. In other words, a total science knows both subjectively and objectively, absolutely and relatively.

The one-sided objective view of science, resulting from an exclusively physical-chemical analytical and experimental method, is contrary to our basic experience of the meaningful processes of evolution and creation. It contradicts the whole reality of life, because it makes a single form of appearance absolute. Therefore, it must be a half-truth. And a half-truth is always, at the same time, half a lie. Indeed, half-truths are the most dangerous lies because, as such, they are most difficult to detect.

Before we are ready to accept such a violation of our normal thought and perception, we must ascertain whether Professor Monod is not using a thought process which has, in the meantime, become reactionary. That is, we must see whether, in biology, we have to use a modern complementary understanding of truth, which is already being used in physics. We may not draw final objective conclusions only from physical-chemical analysis of external appearances and reactions. We must attempt, at the same time, to see connections from the opposite view, from within outward, appraising them subjectively from the inner reality of the process of change.

Since we saw that, besides the purely accidental, mechanical, undirected influence of genetic information, there can be also a goal-directed change of genomes (this possibility is not yet proven experimentally, but it cannot be denied), it is fully legitimate to speak of "creation" as the inner reality of evolution until the contrary is proven.

Not only does physics demand a complementary understanding of reality in answer to contradictory appearances and ideas, but the story of the evolution of nature and of man also does so. The apparent contradictions of faith and science, subject and object, essence and appearance, must be understood simultaneously as a totality in both of these opposite ways of understanding. Thus, reality and truth are not to be understood scientifically alone nor from a religious standpoint alone.

It is one of the great problems of our times that we have forgotten to view reality in a complementary manner, within a totality. However, modern scientific and religious developments now make it possible for us to see things as they are — not only their inner reality or outer surface alone but also their whole dimension of depth.

The Conditions of Human Life

Professor Monod and other researchers claim that it is completely improbable that the evolution of man, which took place once, could be accomplished a second time in the same way. This can be said not only about evolution as such but also about the preservation of existing beings. Not only would genetic prerequisites of evolution have to remain the same, but also the external conditions which made evolution possible would have to remain the same. One need only to consider how many conditions, other than that of time, must be fulfilled and retained, beyond the stage of the first molecule to the final cell, in order to make evolution possible.

A tremendous amount of "chance" must have been involved over a long period of time. For example, on our planet a comparatively small change of temperature could cause entirely new conditions. Even a mere ten-degree loss of warmth could result in an ice age and a prolongation of all chemical and biological processes necessary for the development of higher life. Corresponding rises in temperature destroy the protein molecules and make stability impossible.

If the atmosphere were too heavy, not enough light could penetrate for the evolution of life. If it were too thin, ultraviolet and other rays would destroy the protein bodies and, with them, life. If the proportion of water to land were not three to two, there would be only arid desert land, like that on the moon. If there were too much oxygen in the atmosphere, the protein bodies would not be stable, and if there were too little oxygen, oxidation processes would be difficult. If the earth's axis were not tilted and the revolutions were not somewhat elliptical, there would be no summer and winter, and there would be a much smaller belt of vegetation. If the distance from the earth to the sun were not comparatively constant in each season, climatic conditions could not be guaranteed. If the rotations of the earth were too fast or too slow, there would be undesirable results on our existence. If there were no moon, we would have no tides with their subsequent changes. If the composition and condition of individual elements and atoms were different, there would be insufficient carbon; protein bodies and organic matter could not be formed. These are only a few of many conditions relevant only to protein bodies, to say nothing of the life of plants and animals, or those conditions which lead to the existence and preservation of human life and to a modern culture and civilization.

Can we imagine what would have to happen to plant growth and to the development of living beings in hundreds of millions of years in order to supply sources of energy, of coal and oil, for us! Today, in the pollution problem, we experience how sensitively higher life reacts to the smallest changes. Not only is the evolution from the mutation of the genome to man totally improbable and unrepeatable as a result of change, but also the exterior conditions of evolution do not tolerate "variations in change" without endangering the whole process. Let us consider a small number of conditions, say 100, which must all be present simultaneously over a billion years, in order to keep the protein molecules and genetic information constant. The probability that all conditions could concur a second time and remain constant is at least as small as one's coming up with all sixes if one were to throw one hundred dice at once.

The Probability of the Existence of Human Life on Other Bodies of the Universe Through Chance Is Nil

Seen from blind "chance" alone, it is totally improbable that all the conditions which were present and remained constant on our planet, ultimately making human life possible, would ever again concur in another place in the universe. Whoever accepts blind chance alone as a reason for evolution would have to come to the logical conclusion that there would be one chance in a million for the sun-earth constellation, with all its countless details, to be. And such an earth had to exist first of all, so that further "chance" in connection with water, air, frost, and thawing, wind, sun and rain could come to be from protein bodies. These, in turn, prepared the ground for higher plants.

Crustaceans and insects had to develop from mollusks; from fish came amphibious animals, reptiles, birds and small mammals; from mammals came apes and, finally, man. After a long period of development from the first man came the human being of today. One might well say, "Blind chance must have had a marvelous vision to cause all these things to come to be." In the nucleus of the fertilized protein cell, as in every cell of the human body, at least 10,000 genes, or units of heredity, can be found in the 46 chromosomes. In the nucleus itself (diameter around one thousandth mm) the complete plan for man, that is, the genetic or hereditary information in its smallest atomic detail, is found. Molecular biologists estimate that the sum of this information would be equal in content to at least 2000 volumes with 500 pages each. These would require about 100 meters on a bookshelf.

The storing of this gigantic amount of information in the fertilized protein cell takes place in DNA. One can imagine it in carefully wound tapes in 46 mini-cassettes, representing 46 chromosomes. The width is two millionths mm in length, the total length 1 to 2 m. nucleic acid because they appear in the nucleus. They form two long chains, made up of many billions of nucleotides. These are each made up of one of the bases: Adenin (A), Thymin (T), Guanin (G) and Cytosin (C), abbreviated to P-Z-B. Molecules are the smallest possible part of these.

SCHEMATIC PRESENTATION OF A VERY SMALL SECTION OF A DNA-DOUBLE CHAIN, THE BEARER OF HEREDITARY INFORMATION

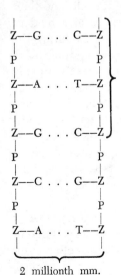

2 millionth mm.

CTC is the "sign" of the code for amino acids, glutamine acids. GTA zB is the "sign for the amino acids, histidine, etc. In normal circumstances, they appear in Z-P-Z-P-Z-cords not on one level, as shown in the schema. They are spiraled around each other like threads in a cord. Through the recurring nucleic acid messengers, the order of the amino acid code signs is carried from the nucleus to the remaining part of the cell. There the proteins are brought together by the various amino acids found in the remaining orders.

To double the genetic information necessary for the doubling of cells, the double chain divides at the dotted points into simple chains. Free nucleotides in the nucleus attach themselves to the simple chains, base to base, and thus complete both simple chains, making them double. As a result of special forms of molecules at the single base, C always joins G, G joins C, and T joins A, etc., so that two new daughter chains, identical to the mother chain, are formed.

As a result of this continuous doubling process, gigantic information comes to exist already in the fertilized protein cell of a newly conceived child. Here we are really concerned with human hereditary information, not with some primitive information of bacteria which lived billions of years ago, as was erroneously held in the biogenetic principle of Haekel.

We agree with the biologist Professor A. Portmann, who in a radio interview with Nobel prizewinner W. Heisenberg, in 1947, said that the question exists now as it did then: *How* did the first order, as it exists in the chromosomes, come about? The same is true of the development of the human cerebrum in the common ancestors of man and perhaps also in the *Australopithecus erectus.*

A computer specialist once explained that the construction of a computer comparable to a human's brain circumference and differentiation, with its ten to twenty billion brain cells and their circuits and connections, would require the space of a modern city. However, since the cerebrum has tripled in size during the course of evolution, a constant upward development would have had to take place in the course of the last million years, with only 50,000 to 80,000 generational changes in a series of developments. At the same time, in each series of every generation, at least one egg or mother cell from which a primitive man developed must have experienced an improved chance mutation of the genome for the development of the cerebrum. However, in order to make a computer the size of a modern city through purely accidental, non-planned mutation, no comparatively small number of generational changes would suffice to explain it.

I would like to emphasize once more that I am not against the idea of "chance" as an expression for which many different reasons can be given. But I am against the pseudo-scientific exaggerations which understand the word "chance" as a mechanical, meaningless happening which is completely blind and not directed by a higher order. It requires much greater faith to believe in blind chance than to believe in God as Creator or in the idea that there can be directed "spiritual" influences and impulses on the genome. These impulses improve the quality of life or the ability to adjust to surroundings. They can come from a being's will to life, as well as from a general tendency toward a higher development. The sentences "And God said, 'Let there be . . .' and there was" (v.9) and " 'Let the earth (matter) bring forth . . .' " refer to the same reason for general evolution and are entirely consistent with modern scientific thought about the evolution of man. Social changes through spiritual inspiration are undisputed in the history of man.

Basically, however, it is not so decisive which type of faith motivates one's decisions if we are concerned with the shocking price expended in order to make our existence possible. A thinking person really can be only reverently amazed and completely awed by it!

Indeed, it seems as if the understanding of the incomprehensible complication of evolution and of our own existence could lead once more to a Copernican turning point.

At the time of Copernicus, man was forced out of the center of the world by a purely quantitative view of the world, of the earth and of his own little existence when he learned that the sun did not revolve around the earth, but *vice versa*. We must recognize that it is completely improbable, from the point of view of the chance theory of evolution as well as from a religious view, that the same evolution could repeat itself somewhere else in the universe in the same way. We, therefore, have a right to conclude that a world had to exist in order to permit the completely improbable "chance" for man to exist. In our solar system man is, in any event, the qualitatively best-developed and last-appearing being who can be regarded as the last step in evolution and, therefore, also as the "goal of evolution." The purely quantitative manner of thinking during the last centuries must be complemented by qualitative thinking of the goal of evolution. We must admit that the existence of man, and especially the spiritual and cultural development of a free personality in a community of free men, is the greatest mystery and miracle we know.

In this connection Konrad Lorenz wrote, "We are the climax of all that which the greatest builders of change on earth have reached until now. We are their 'last cry' but definitely not their last word . . ." This view, which consciously includes also a subjective appreciation, thus challenging Professor Monod's animism, cannot be disregarded even from a purely objective approach to reality.

APPENDIX II

With the permission of the authors I quote from a book of H. D. Dossenbach and E. M. Buehrer, published by C. J. Bucher, about the flights, practices, adaptability and distribution of the cow heron. They write:

"A bird which is so adventurous is naturally an ideal object for the study of a behaviorist. Otto Koenig caught several young cow herons in North America, took them to his research station on Mount Wilhelmine near Vienna and then let them fly. In the fall they were caught, put into a heated area, and in the spring they were moved into a newly-built open cage. In the meantime something surprising happened. The one-year-old birds had already gotten the cinnamon-brown brooding feathers. Herons, living in the freedom of nature, get these feathers only in the second year and as a rule also become capable of reproduction only then. After a few days a pair began to build a nest. A week later the first pale blue egg, upon which both mates sat alternatingly, appeared. After two-day intervals more eggs appeared. Finally, the first cow heron was born in captivity. The surroundings of such captivity can never be the same as those found in the freedom of nature. No time is consumed in hunting for food or searching for nesting materials because all that the birds need is abundantly at hand. This affluence soon had an impressive effect on the behavior of the cow heron.

"In the freedom of nature the growing young herons are forced to find their own food because of the long absences of their hunting parents in the large areas in which they live. In this way the young learn to hunt and soon become independent. The young birds' urge to wander causes them to move to other areas and so they instinctively avoid inbreeding. Here on Mount Wilhelmine the parents were always there to feed their young, which had no opportunity to become independent and stayed around their parents. Neither did the family separate during the next breeding period. Something happened now which could never have happened in the freedom of nature. Within the family every male

mated every female according to whim. All eggs were laid into a
common nest upon which all wanted to sit. They constantly relieved each other, and often three birds sat on the nest at the same
time, sitting on top of each other. The young of the year before
still begged their parents for, and received, food, which they, in
turn, gave their own young. The courtship and mating ceremonies,
otherwise so complicated, were shortened. There was no need to
learn to know each other through courtship rites, for the marriage
partner was the father, brother or son. Thus the courtship ceremonies were used less and less and finally dropped altogether.

"In the following spring this 'degeneration, resulting from
affluence' continued. Various families of the colony began to merge
into larger families in which every male mated every female, so
that nothing remained of the former strict monogamous marriages.
Polygamy reigned instead. How much this way of life disturbed
the regular, usual behavior of the birds could best be seen in the
constantly declining birth rate. Eggs were cast out because of
constant activity; young were overfed and finally oppressed.

"Parallels to the development of human beings in our modern
civilization cannot be mistaken here. This is an unusually instruc-
tive example for the behaviorist who compares the behavior of
animals and human beings."

APPENDIX III

"*Humanae Vitae* and the New Sexuality"

(An article by Peter Riga published in *Triumph*, October, 1973)

The question of the relationship between sexuality and procreation is both delicate and complex. But what is very clear today is that a swelling alliance of diverse forces views this relationship, in any form, as a positive curse. Gay liberation, lesbianism, the playboy philosophers, the radical women liberationists — all have this in common. They are all conducting a frontal attack on a relationship that has been historically regarded as natural, and therefore necessary. Yet if there *is* a natural relationship between sexuality and procreation, i.e., one necessary for human integration, then these various manifestations of the new sexuality which today are not only demanding a hearing from our compassion and understanding, but are agitating for recognition by society at large as "sexual alternatives," are truly monstrous. They are, in reality, human perversions.

The success of all these movements depends entirely on their ability to separate sexuality from procreation. If they are successful, there will remain no logical reason why lesbianism should not be considered the moral equivalent of monogamous and faithful marriage, why homosexuality should not be "open" to the same "free choice" as a constant, committed and loyal heterosexual relationship, that is, marriage. In short, if the relationship between sexuality and procreation is only tenuous or accidental, then a homosexual "marriage" has indeed the same claim to validity and respect as a true marriage.

This is why the relationship between sexuality and procreation is such a crucial question, and why it must be faced squarely and boldly. It is the rock bottom question which Paul VI dealt with in his much derided encyclical *Humanae Vitae*, and it has become even more pressing today as the movements I mention gain a more and more favorable hearing, especially under pressure from the "overpopulation" craze; and as monogamous and permanent marriage is openly mocked as a "restraint" on human possibilities and experience.

I do not propose to discuss the motives of these groups — of gays, liberationists, playboys, playgirls. That is always a dangerous thing to do, since we cannot enter into the hearts and consciences of others. It is also a waste of time. What must be discussed is not the motives of people but their actions and the logical consequences of these actions on the lives of people, on a whole culture and on the whole future of the relationship between the sexes.

The sexual in man and woman is not simply some zone of the body which can be localized. In spite of the modern usage, human sexuality is infinitely more than copulation. It is the sexual which helps open man and woman to each other — which openness is the very basis of the relationship itself. The sexual in man is a call, a vocation, to go out of the self to the other. By answering the call, a person can break the bonds of aloneness and solitude and can thereby relate to another. This relationship is the basis of family and community, which in turn allow the person to relate to a past and above all to a future

The biological substratum in this relationship is basic and cannot be denied, except in the mind. The woman feels this truth more vividly than the man, as a sort of total vibration. The knowledge of the sexual in her biology is what the scholastics would call "ontological"; it is stamped on her very being. Her maternal instinct is profoundly written in her biology, and she is monthly reminded of this deep sexual role which she cannot escape. The indelible sexual stamp on her biology naturally and directly relates her to a potential new life, to its beginning, its nurture, its conservation. She is there when a baby is conceived, when it grows, when it is born, when it feeds from her, and when it develops from absolute helplessness to physical and emotional stability.

The male's sexuality is largely dependent on that of the woman because, from a biological point of view, his relationship with a child is tenuous at best. The male's diffuse energies become purposeful and integrated when a culture specifies his responsibility to protect and support the woman he has chosen, their offspring and their family life. When these roles in family life break down, the male becomes predator of human relations without commitment and stability, with the result that his own sexual identity is lost in the irresponsibility of playboyism of the "find 'em and forget 'em" variety.

The male in most known societies has had to "prove" his masculinity or virility. There have been a variety of methods — killing an enemy in battle, enduring various painful ordeals, killing some wild animal, building a house, finding and holding a "job." But while males must thus demonstrate their sexual worth, females never have to do this in any society with which we are historically acquainted. As we have noted, the woman's biology, with its monthly reminders, is the *per se* determinant of her destiny and of her role in the supreme matter of family life, on which the very future of the tribe or society rests. Where these roles are deeply disrupted — as is happening today, thanks in large part to the feminist movement's "equalizing" agitation — then both male and female are set adrift, family life is jeopardized or destroyed, as is the very relationship between the sexes.

In marriage, the institution itself is of infinitely more importance than the love relationship — at least from the point of view of the species. Marriage attracts men and women, explicitly or implicitly, for the purpose of having children, and of giving these new persons a future and a history. Thus the basic truth of Christian tradition: marriage has as its primary, i.e., indispensable, end, the begetting and education of children. Certainly, this purpose should be pursued in a context of love and in a relationship between two persons of equal dignity — but whose relationship is that of *male and female*. This is why it is the business of any healthy and decent society to protect and encourage that monogamous and committed relationship in cultural patterns and legislation. When a society refuses to do so — when it makes the sexual aberrations of homosexuality, common law marriage, and extramarital sex, the equivalent of monogamous marriage — then it conspires to destroy healthy sexual relationships between men and women and consequently the institution of marriage. If this is allowed to continue unchecked, then virtual suicide of the sexes as well as of *that* society is assured.

We are faced today precisely with this situation in a society which encourages pornography, playboy-girlism, homosexuality and lesbianism, as well as the corrosion and degeneration of natural sexual roles by the new feminism. And at the bottom of this massive cultural attack on monogamous and committed sexual love is precisely the separation — considered to be a "right" by most segments of American society — of procreation from sexuality in the relationship between the sexes.

I am not of course suggesting that women should not develop all of their God-given talents and make their unique contribution to society and to the enrichment of its culture. What must be firmly resisted is the attempt by feminists and others to disparage the most important role a woman has, both in family life and as it affects the human race — namely, that of nurturess of children. This disparagement is written all over the feminist literature. Child-rearing and domesticity are "dull," "non-expanding," "constricting;" they deny the "natural right" of woman to find her place alongside man in the world of business and the professions. This attack on the supreme maternal role of woman must be resisted at all costs because it is basically anti-human and anti-Christian. In reality, it is a new form of an old heresy, Manichaeism: the sexual is really dirty, and stands for passing eroticism and pleasure with no prolonged commitment of self in enduring love which we call marriage. No wonder the new feminists look with great satisfaction on massive day-care centers, *in vitro* and AID fertilization, etc.; with such de-humanizing devices, the new Manichaeism can be practiced with an absolute minimum of domesticity, family life and human commitment in enduring and monogamous marriage. In short, what we find at the heart of all the new sexuality movements is a direct attack on Christian marriage. They all hold out the cynical and irresponsible delights of easy sex, in disparagement and mockery of monogamous and committed sexual marriage. The cancerous and abnormal cells in the body of this society now make the outlandish and unhistorical claim that it is they who are healthy while the natural organisms of society are diseased. Evil is now good, and good evil.

The reality of the matter is that human sexuality has no meaning — it becomes sterile, it has no history or future — without married sexual life in a family. Sexual acts performed with a variety of partners, the half-crazed desire on the part of so many to study the latest sex manuals on the various positions and techniques for achieving the ultimate in pleasurable orgasms — such behavior can develop no history for a true personal relationship; and the sexual appetite proves insatiable precisely because there is no such history of growth between two human beings. Such growth can take place only within a context of committed marital love where the sexual act is not simply an erotic experience (it is that also) but, more importantly, is part of a dynamic unfolding of a history between two loving persons.

Moreover, acts which seek directly to separate sexuality from procreation have no future, and are therefore doubly sterile. They enter into no transcendent endeavor, which is precisely what the family is all about. Marriage and its necessary consequence, the family, is a transcendent relationship in which two persons engage themselves and seek to perfect themselves in a common endeavor that reaches outside of the relationship — to new life, to the future of the human race, to God's glory. There is no more important or vital work among men than this. And since the various forms of the new sexuality destroy family life and man's transcendence at its root, they must be seen for the perversions they really are. No amount of compassion for the plight of homosexuals — and the plight is quite real — must be allowed to obscure what homosexuality and its counterparts truly are and what they entail. The practices associated with the stud, the playboy-girl, the contraceptive marriage, the homosexual-lesbian, all lack both a history and a future, and are therefore sterile. Is not insistent but purposeless copulation a definition of sterility? And sex is purposeless when separated from love, commitment and openness to life — which are the very definition of monogamous Christian marriage.

I have referred to contraception, and this is of course the dominant form of the perversion of sexuality that separates sexuality from procreation, and the form that was the explicit subject of *Humanae Vitae*. It is true that Catholic teaching permits the spacing and limiting of offspring for a variety of reasons, and has approved the methods of self-denial and rhythm, which cooperate with man's natural biology. But what we are addressing ourselves to here is a real "contraceptive mentality" which radically separates the sexual from the procreative as a "right" of every couple, whether in or out of marriage. The assertion of this alleged right, which is almost totally accepted in our society, is the basic explanation for the widespread approval for the perversions discussed above. And there should be no illusion in anyone's mind that as we decide whether to accept or reject the contraceptive mentality, we decide radically how we conceive the whole human sexual dynamism.

The contraceptive mentality, I maintain, radically contradicts the inner syntax of human sexuality itself and therefore ultimately destroys the humanity of the people who insistently act upon it. The very essence of the sex act, from a biological point of view, is procreative. We must clearly understand — under pain of sharing the new Manichaeism — that man's biological substratum is an essential dimension of him, and that radical separation from it disintegrates him at his basic root. This is above all true of the woman. The consequences of "free sex" for her are especially disastrous, since what she thereby denies is an essential and deeply rooted dimension of her very being. That is why abortion is basically an attack not only on her child but on herself.

Thus, the sexual act is an act of *human* affirmation and commitment. It is also a transcendent reality as an affirmation of a man's own, as well as his race's, future. Without a future, man is closed in upon himself in a form of implicit sexual despair because his sexuality is going nowhere in spite of multiplied sexual acts. Such sexual activity might have a history — i.e., a relationship of real love — but if it is now in no way associated with at least an implicit desire for children, it lacks the structure of futurity and is therefore *per se* a destructive sexual experience between these two people.

The foregoing analysis, I repeat, is derived from the structure or syntax of the sexual act itself, not merely from the loving relationship between the couple. The argument rests, therefore, not on psychology but, more profoundly, on the structure or ontology of the act itself, which man must respect if he is to remain whole and healthy.

It should be clear, then, that all sexual aberrations mentioned participate directly in the disintegration of human sexuality. They are a single voice in seeking, in one way or another, to separate the exercise of human sexuality from its procreative function. And let us not underestimate the effect of this voice: the array of pressures, especially in the mass media, against Christian marriage and family life is simply horrendous to contemplate; indeed it is problematic at best whether the healthy cells of Christian families and marriages will long be able to withstand these pressures. In the words of George Gilder: "The first and most important step in restoring a sense of order and purpose and community is to re-establish the social pressures and cultural biases in favor of durable monogamous love and marriage."

How embarrassing, unfortunately, for many Catholics that Pope Paul VI has proved to be absolutely correct in his analysis of the modern sexual situation in *Humanae Vitae*. It is embarrassing for the theologians as well; and, for what it is worth, I ask pardon for not seeing more clearly before this.

APPENDIX IV

"We Forgive and Ask Forgiveness"

We are concerned, in no way, with a purely ecclesiastical principle, but with a fundamental law of life. This is very obvious in the European question, namely, how can we achieve a genuine cleansing of our relationship with people in Eastern Europe, especially with the Poles, in order to avoid new enmities and much worse destruction in the end? How is genuine peace possible between us?

Can peace be achieved solely by the recognition of the Oder-Neisse boundary, without any stipulations, but with the implied justification of the expulsion and mass murder of Germans who lived there many centuries? Could we officially declare this right? Or should we have insisted on our right and demanded that this land become German again, although we know that this could be realized, at most, through war? What would change an external agreement in which no Pole believes, because neither he nor his people were ever prepared to give up even a foot of Polish land? Must the Poles not regard us as hypocrites and ignoble sneaks if we capitulate out of fear? Genuine peace, however, assumes complete mutual trust as its foundation. It can come about only if we admit the injustices we perpetrated against the Poles and ask forgiveness. Conversely, the same is true for the Poles.

When the Archbishop of Breslau said, "We forgive and beg forgiveness," he had to retract his words due to the wrong reaction of Germans. Yet, for us, there is only one consideration: that common spiritual heritage which Polish and German knights who fought and died under the Cross near Liegnitz and Vienna once defended against the Mongols and Turks. When hundreds of thousands of Poles cried, "We forgive!" at the millesimal anniversary in Tschenstochau, the moment would have been right for a similar action on our part. Only the forgiveness of guilt on both sides can lead to a rebirth of Polish and German cooperation, after all the crimes and bloodshed of the past! A new heart is a prerequisite for peace between our peoples. Why should men who have sinned thus against each other, and suffered so much at the hands of each other, not come to a new relationship through mutual forgiveness? This new relationship would be deeper and more indestructible than anything they ever experienced before. Hunger for power, nationalism and hatred drove them into deadly enmity. If peace would come about, all European boundaries could be removed and we could form a united Europe, without later calling the injustice of the past justice.

We Germans surely ought to make a start and accept the outstretched hands of those Poles who believe they can make a new start from the message of the Cross and who are waiting for our answer. Peace does not consist in treaties and explanations on paper, but in hearts ready for change, in new intentions, and in the purification of relationships with God and neighbor, as the focal point of our human and national existence.

This restoration of relationships is the Church's most important concern and mission. Great human problems must be seen, first and always, from the point of view of the relationship between man and God. Constantly, we must be concerned about keeping this relationship free from disturbances, testing the consequences of definite types of conduct in regard to it and, finally, deciding from a God-centered vantage point what is right and what is wrong.

APPENDIX V

Yesterday's Science, Today's Ideological Error: Thoughts on Contemporary Religious Instruction

Religious instruction has for its content faith in God and the question of man's relationship to God.

In our day educators are being forced to spend more and more time in introducing the student to an acquaintance with the results of modern scientific research.

Science proceeds with the help of hypotheses. The purpose of a hypothesis is to explain certain phenomena and interrelationships in reality around us as observed by means of modern technical instruments and methods. The fewer the contradictions a hypothesis contains and the more it can be confirmed by experiment and experience, the more valid it seems to be and the more in conformity with the truth.

The true scientist will therefore always choose as his working hypothesis the theory that his view explains, without inconsistency, the greatest range of phenomena. He always abandons hypotheses when they are at odds with known reality or do not enable him to explore the phenomena further. A hypothesis, like a thesis, is an unproved assumption, a belief that is assumed for the sake of further work but is not itself a piece of scientific knowledge. We cannot imagine scientific advances being made without the help of hypotheses.

Since many hypotheses about reality and its phenomena are, in the last analysis, beliefs, the communication of such hypotheses to students becomes in fact the communication of a world view that in many cases has some positive or negative connection with the question of God. Hypotheses that are suggested by a materialistic picture of the world and that proceed (for example) from the premise that only what the chemist and physicist can measure is real, stand in contradiction to belief in God and either destroy that belief or at least lead to a schizoid frame of mind.

In a pluralistic school, it is entirely up to the individual teacher what interpretation he gives of the phenomena and facts that are dealt with in science, that is, what kind of hypothesis he applies in order to explain reality.

Consequently, it depends entirely on chance or on the good will of a teacher whether when it comes to the fundamental and decisive hypotheses and the world-view behind them, the student is presented with a way of interpreting phenomena that does not exclude the existence of God but "is open to God."

It is pointless to talk to the younger generation about the Bible if their belief in God is being undermined by the picture of the world that is communicated to them by their study of other subjects, or if belief in God is made to seem a reactionary superstition that cannot stand up to scientific examination. Any successful religious instruction will therefore depend on whether the teacher manages to give the student an overall picture in which the knowledge communicated by revelation and the knowledge achieved by science are complementary.

If the teacher of religion is to be able to do this, he must have accurate knowledge of the most important hypotheses now being used and of the attempts being made to explain scientific data and phenomena. More than that, he must be in a position to provide his students with intellectual alternatives to the most important materialistic hypotheses and thus to make belief in God an intellectual possibility. (This process has nothing to do with offering proofs for the existence of God; it is simply a matter of showing that many supposed proofs of a pseudoscientific kind are really an expression of beliefs inspired by a materialistic ideology, and of proposing other hypotheses that are not incompatible with belief in God.) We shall now list some of the hypotheses that are being communicated these days through instruction in physics, chemistry, biology, psychology, sexuality, sociology, scientific history, etc., and that are materialistically inspired and oriented, although very probably they are scientifically untenable and can readily be replaced by more satisfactory hypotheses which do not exclude God.

The materialist faith makes use of the following hypotheses:

1. Matter alone is real; it is eternal and immutable.

Alfred Rust, *Handwerkliches Koennen und Lebensweise des Steinzeit-menschen.* Mannheimer Forum 1973/1974.

Dossenbach und Buehrer, *Von Liebe und Ehe der Voegel.* Verlag C. J. Bucher, Lucerne. 1974.

Pasqual Jordan, *Naturwissenschaft vor der religioesen Frage.* Stallin Verlag. 1970.

H. G. Studnitz, *Ist Gott Mitlaeufer?* Seewaldverlag. 1969.

Peter Howard, *Amerika braucht eine Ideologie.* Verlag Deutscher Buchdienst.

Pasqual Jordan, *Naturwissenschaft und christlicher Glaube.* 1970.

Pope Paul VI, *Zusatzerklaerung zur Enzyklika* Humanae Vitae. 1968.

Paul Roemhild, *Weltbild und Glaube.* Evang. Luth. Volkshochschule Alexandersbad. 1970.

Paul Roemhild, *Am Anfang schuf Gott Himmel und Erde.* Schoepfung und Naturwissenschaft. Alexandersbader Hefte, 1972.

Ernst Ell, *Dynamische Sexualmoral.* Benziger Verlag. 1972.

W. Schoellgen, *Moral fragwuerdig.* Roborverlag Hueckeswagen. 1967.

Kurt Port, *Sexdiktatur.* Portverlag, Esslingen/N. 1972.

Dr. and Mrs. Willke, *Handbook on Abortion.* Hiltz Publishing Co., Cincinnati, Ohio. 1973.

Dr. John Billings, *Natural Family Planning.* The Liturgical Press, Collegeville, Minnesota. 1973.

M. R. Joyce and R. E. Joyce, *New Dynamics in Sexual Love.* The Liturgical Press, Collegeville, Minnesota. 1970.

Dr. med. Sievers, *Natur und Enzyklika.* Johann Wilhelm Naumann Verlag, Wuerzburg. 1969.

Dr. med. Sievers, *Wege zur natuerlichen Empfaengnisverhuetung.* Johann Wilhelm Naumann Verlag, Wuerzburg. 1969.

Irmela Hoffman, *Lebensiaenglich.* Aussaat Verlag, Wuppertal. 1972.

Klaus Bockmuehl, *Atheismus in der Christenheit.* Aussaat Verlag. 1969.

Joerg Gutzwiller, *Mensch Gott Welt.* Theolog. Verlag, Zuerich. 1971.

Erwin Straus, *Psychologie der menschlichenWelt.* Gesammelte Schriften. Springer Verlag Goettinger. 1960.

Balthasar Staehelin, *Urvertrauen und zweite Wirklichkeit.* Editio Academica Zuerich. 1973.

Memorandum der Europaeischen Aerzteaktion an die Europaeischen Parlamente zur Abtreibungsfrage. Verlag Aktion Ulm 70. Ulm, Postfach 672. 1973.

Gemeinsame Erklaerung der Moraltheologen der Bundesrepublik Deutschland v. 27.4.1974.

Protokolle Deutscher Bundestag, Pornographiehearing. November 1971.

Demokratie und Freie Liebe, Denkschrift von 140 schwedischen Aerzten an den Koenig. Deutsche Tagespost, Wuerzburg, 8.1.1966.

In a pluralistic school, it is entirely up to the individual teacher what interpretation he gives of the phenomena and facts that are dealt with in science, that is, what kind of hypothesis he applies in order to explain reality.

Consequently, it depends entirely on chance or on the good will of a teacher whether when it comes to the fundamental and decisive hypotheses and the world-view behind them, the student is presented with a way of interpreting phenomena that does not exclude the existence of God but "is open to God."

It is pointless to talk to the younger generation about the Bible if their belief in God is being undermined by the picture of the world that is communicated to them by their study of other subjects, or if belief in God is made to seem a reactionary superstition that cannot stand up to scientific examination. Any successful religious instruction will therefore depend on whether the teacher manages to give the student an overall picture in which the knowledge communicated by revelation and the knowledge achieved by science are complementary.

If the teacher of religion is to be able to do this, he must have accurate knowledge of the most important hypotheses now being used and of the attempts being made to explain scientific data and phenomena. More than that, he must be in a position to provide his students with intellectual alternatives to the most important materialistic hypotheses and thus to make belief in God an intellectual possibility. (This process has nothing to do with offering proofs for the existence of God; it is simply a matter of showing that many supposed proofs of a pseudoscientific kind are really an expression of beliefs inspired by a materialistic ideology, and of proposing other hypotheses that are not incompatible with belief in God.) We shall now list some of the hypotheses that are being communicated these days through instruction in physics, chemistry, biology, psychology, sexuality, sociology, scientific history, etc., and that are materialistically inspired and oriented, although very probably they are scientifically untenable and can readily be replaced by more satisfactory hypotheses which do not exclude God.

The materialist faith makes use of the following hypotheses:

1. Matter alone is real; it is eternal and immutable.

2. The universe is infinite and has neither beginning nor end.

3. The spirit and soul of man are simply a projection and function of the material elements that make up the human body.

4. The laws governing the evolution of life are predetermined by matter.

5. Nothing is real but the matter that is dealt with by the chemist and the physicist; nothing exists but what is measurable and experimentally demonstrable.

6. Man and the whole of animate nature are simply a product of accidental changes in the conditions which govern the chemical and physical processes of matter. They result especially from accidental mutations in the genetic material and in the accompanying selection of the fittest through the inevitable struggle for existence. In all this, Professor J. Monod (*Chance and Necessity: An Essay in the Natural Philosophy of Modern Biology*, translated by A. Wainhouse; New York: Knopf, 1971) assumes that everything is the result of blind chance, whereas Marxist theoreticians claim that "as yet unknown laws" are at work, causing "a sudden change in quality through changes in quantity." The example always given is the leap involved in the qualitative change of water into steam.

7. The individual human being repeats the complete evolutionary process from unicellular living thing, through sea urchin, fish, and mammal, to man (Haeckel's biogenetic principle). This in turn is proof that evolution is universal throughout nature.

8. The history of mankind as a whole is the history simply of mankind's material foundations and drives. The decisive factors in this history are the law of the transformation of quantity into quality, as applied in the area of the means and relations of production, and, secondly, the struggle for these means (the class struggle). In the last analysis, then, all history is nothing but the history of the class struggle for possession of raw materials and the means of production.

9. The natural laws discovered by physics and chemistry are absolute laws. Biological and spiritual-moral laws, on the contrary, are simply a product of the material and economic substructure; in other words, they are "class laws" meant for the oppression of the exploited by the exploiter.

a superior organism and a higher level of existence. Consequently, only some of the "laws of evolution" are contained in the material elements.

4. Information and inspiration (in the sense given these words above) frequently make use of a chemico-physical and therefore quantitatively measurable base. They are not, however, completely identical with this base. As modern parapsychology and our daily experience show, there can be information and inspiration without any chemico-physical go-between. Telepathy, thought transference, and hypnosis do not make use of electromagnetic waves or any other discernible vehicle of information.

5. Consequently, the fifth point in the overall materialist hypothesis — namely, that nothing is real but the matter that can be measured by the chemist and the physicist — becomes an arbitrary belief, and thus a superstition, since it lacks any demonstrable scientific foundation.

6. Selection effected through struggle is a basic biological and intellectual law. It is also a law of the New Testament (many are called, but few are chosen). On the other hand, the attempt to explain evolution solely through accidental mutations represents an unscientific act of faith that is inspired by materialism; the same must be said of the alternative explanation, that evolution follows "as yet unknown laws" (Stalin). Once our daily experience has acquainted us with information and inspiration as forces that shape and organize our daily life and are not to be adequately explained in terms of chance or mechanics or chemico-physical processes, there is no longer any reason for forcing upon the realm of cells, molecules, and elementary parts an explanation that is mechanistic or appeals to pure chance. Nor is there any reason for not assuming that even at these rudimentary levels the laws of information and inspiration are at work.

The claim that a higher genetic level arises solely through an accidental mutation or through a leaplike mutation in accordance with "as yet unknown laws" (and thus without any directedness) is therefore a faith-inspired hypothesis that has no scientific proof behind it and is even contrary to experience. Precisely because of its lack of probability, such a hypothesis is a piece of pseudo-scientific superstition. In no case can the possibility be excluded that there are genetic changes and mutations of the hereditary material, that is, a change of information, which occur through inspiration. For there can be no serious doubt today that elementary parts, atoms, molecules, cells and organs can react to immaterial commands and impulses. This means in turn that modern natural science presents no barrier to explaining miracles, as found in the Bible, through inspiration, just as creation itself is thus explicable.

I must insist once again: there is no question of using science to prove the miracles of the Bible or creation by God. What we can do, however, is to eliminate the contradictions which make miracles and creation inconceivable from the viewpoint of natural science.

When Marxists use the example of the change of fluid water into gaseous H_2O as grounds for claiming a qualitative transformation of social processes through quantitative changes, and thus as a justification for their bloody revolutions, this is either a grotesque error or a deliberate act of deception. It is simply astonishing that anyone should be able nowadays to get hundreds of millions of supposedly rational human beings to accept this sort of nonsense as "science."

For, there is no quantity that is not at the same time a quality. Consequently, there is no transformation of quantity into quality but only a change from one quality to another. You can increase the quantity of a single drop of water by adding a whole ocean to it, and there will be no change in the state of H_2O. The three states of H_2O depend on the energy at work in each, and the three states are reversible as well. The basic Marxist principle is thus not scientific at all; at best it is a deception practiced on the people. Modern religious instruction should be bringing such lies to light in the interests of the truth.

7. Modern molecular biology and embryology have shown the biogenetic principle to be a bit of pious wishful thinking or even trickery. From the very first moment, a human being has never been an amoeba, a sea urchin, a fish, or a simple mammal. The first cell resulting from the fusion of egg and sperm has the unique and specifically human set of forty-six chromosomes and is at every point a human cell, just as steam, water, and ice are always H_2O

despite the variation of states and phenomena. At no point does man have gills or fur or a tail, as Ernst Haeckel assumed.

The fact that Haeckel in attempting to prove his theory and hypothesis passed off the embryo of a dog as the embryo of a human being shows how much the wish, begotten by a world view, was father to the thought and the hypothesis. The teacher of religion must, when necessary, correct the claims made in textbooks and schoolbooks that during the first three months a human being is "a kind of cluster of cells," and so forth. The uniqueness of the human germ cells and the absence of any genetic forms of transition to other types of animal are a hitherto unanswered argument against the thesis of universal evolution through accidental mutation of the genetic material.

8. As a representation of history, historical materialism, which is based on half-truths and wishful thinking, is likewise no longer a defensible hypothesis. Its internal contradictions cannot be eliminated. For one thing, the motivations by which Jesus Christ and his disciples initiated the most revolutionary process known to the history of mankind had not the slightest thing to do with the means and relations of production, but were the result of inspiration and incarnation. The researches and discoveries of a Johannes Kepler and numerous other savants were not inspired by economic considerations but were in fact often linked to economic drawbacks. The economic progress in methods of production that led to industrialization presupposed the discovery of physical and chemical laws that were not the product of class struggles or special views on the economy. We now know that many great discoveries and inventions resulted from sudden ideas and an intuitive grasp of inner connections, and were not always the fruit of logical analysis. No one can deny, therefore, that inspiration plays an essential role in history.

It is false, too, to act on the supposition that the private possession of the means of production is incompatible with the unselfish use of this economic potential to create jobs and to serve and help others. It is false that anyone who has money must automatically be exploiting others. In reality, there are many examples to the contrary, of men who felt the responsible disposal of property to be God's commission to them and who therefore did remarkable things for their fellow men. Over against such people we have Joseph Stalin, the one time hero and prototype of a communistic society, who lived in a country that had eliminated the private possession of the means of production and who misused his power over economic life and the State in order to exploit and oppress the Russian people in the worst possible way. The economic factor is by no means dependent for its operation in history on the "system"; in the last analysis its operation depends rather on the intellectual, moral and religious outlook and decisions of those who control it.

9. The laws of physics have proved to be regularities which are observed by the parts whose interrelationships they regulate, not in an absolute way but only within the limits of statistical probability. The capacity of the elemental parts of matter to react to non-material impulses is being discussed today and cannot be denied in principle. Consequently, most of the biblical miracles become conceivable and need not be regarded as suspensions of natural laws; they may be understood rather as examples of the control of the elements of nature by what is non-material.

The purpose of the laws of nature is to make possible and to conserve the higher forms of organization of living things and the higher stages of existence. For atoms, molecules, cells, organs, and organisms can perdure in existence only if the parts of which they are composed relate to each other according to certain physical, chemical, and biological regularities. The laws seem to be absolute at all these levels, but in boundary situations the observance of the laws cannot be foreseen as beyond the possibility of exception. In certain situations the part possesses a kind of freedom.

The same holds for the organisms of human society and for their capacity to perdure. Higher social organisms can exist only if individual men and particular groups relate to one another in accordance with clear intellectual and moral norms. In the abstract these norms are absolute and independent of individuals, nations, classes, and races, for they derive from the ideal picture of the social organism's health and ability to function. It can be said of these norms that individuals and groups never follow them without exception, yet without such norms there can be no human society and culture.

The claim of dialectical materialism that spiritual and moral laws are simply the product of economic relationships and power structures proves to be false. The hypothesis is thus a pseudo-scientific superstition.

Class struggle and revolution are rather the result of the non-observance and violation of the absolute moral norms governing human society, as individuals, families, nations, classes, and races replace these laws and norms of action with arbitrary behavior and a rejection of law. One task of religious instruction is to bring out the essential identity of these lifegiving natural laws of society with the ethical norms of the Bible. The stupidity of claiming that there should be "lawless spaces," in which private conscience determines its own norms, is clear from the fact that nowhere in nature do we find "lawless" areas.

10. The view that there are no universally binding norms of right and wrong, because various peoples follow a variety of customs and "moralities," is in contradiction to our experience of the development of norms in the technological, scientific, and economic areas. The diversity, inaccuracy, and relativity of the old weights and measures, written characters, number systems, and so forth, led to their being dropped. No one concluded, however, that because these old norms were inadequate for modern development, we should opt for having no norms and laws. Instead, the old weights and measures were replaced by universal and absolute measures and norms which everyone agreed to accept. This paved the way for the rise of a scientific, technological, and economic organism on a worldwide scale. Modern instruments of measurement made possible increasingly accurate results, close to perfection.

Similar observations must be made with regard to paving the way for a worldwide political, ideological, and juridical organism. A future society that will function effectively is inconceivable apart from absolute and universally binding norms of action. Since the norms are valid for individuals, families, businesses, communities, peoples, classes, races, and all mankind, and since all the organs of collective decision, the parliaments, and the governments, and so on must make their decisions in accordance with these norms, and are capable of acting in the light of them, we can indeed speak of a "collective conscience" for these "juridical persons." It is also possible for whole collectivities, via their decision-making bodies, to act contrary to the higher laws or, in religious language, to make decisions contrary to God's will and plan and thus to "sin."

Conscience is a sure knowledge of the existence of ways of acting that are necessary for the life of a community (Do unto others as you would have them do unto you!). The sense of shame, moreover, is by no means an artificial acquisition. We can see intimations of it even in the higher animals, as for example the dolphin. It is closely connected with personality development, serving as a protective reflex against collectivization and socialization. This is true especially of the woman: nakedness turns her into a spectacle and the possession of males generally; as a result her personality cannot develop because she is not permitted to withdraw into privacy and to defend herself against importunate intrusions and against the occupation and subjection of her body and person by the thoughts and eyes of others. Education for motherhood, and for fatherhood too, requires that the person be able to distance herself, or himself, from others. Unless the individual can stand off and distinguish himself clearly from others, he becomes an apathetic lump.

Without a sense of shame there will be no continence prior to marriage and no lifelong marriage. Without sexual discipline, moreover, there will be no higher cultural development and certainly no belief in God (cf. I. D. Unwin, *Sex and Culture*, Oxford University Press). The repression of the sense of shame is always paid for by a loss of sexual discipline and cultural decadence.

10-A. The environmental theory held that intelligence, character, and the ability to succeed are the product of education, circumstances, class, and environment. It was this theory that led Lenin to say: every washerwoman must be so educated that she could govern a State if need be. Another consequence of the theory is the demand in the German Democratic Republic that the children of workers should be sent to the universities before anyone else and that the children of clergymen (for example) should be excluded from them.

All this represents an extreme reaction to Nazism — as though racial differences were completely irrelevant. Equality of opportunity, as though nature had made all men fully equal; radical democratization in every area of life, as though all were equally competent to form opinions and pass judgment and equally able to share responsibility in every area; discrimination against outstanding accomplishments and the "drive to accomplish": these and many other destructive positions are direct consequences of the pseudoscientific hypothesis embodied in pedagogical environmentalism.

Happily, this question, which Hitler's crimes had made taboo for us Germans, has now been dealt with in detail by a Jewish professor of psychology, H. J. Eysenck. Doctor Eysenck sums up the results of the research that has been done, and shows that the I. Q. differs not only from individual to individual but from one social stratum to another and from one race to another. He sees the inheritance factor and the education factor related in an 80:20 ratio; that is, inheritance is four times more influential than education. This means that without the proper genetic basis a person will be unable to achieve superior accomplishments despite educational programs and social or socialistic measures. Eysenck also shows that the very effort to make everyone equal has the effect in the long run of preventing high achievements by individual and society.

The genetic-biological factor must thus be set alongside the spiritual-moral factor as decisive for historical development. The former must also be acknowledged as prior to, or more important than, the economic-material factor. The "scientific" hypothesis of dialectical and historical materialism that environment and relations of production are all-determining is a lie, made up of two-thirds falsehood and one-third truth. The teacher of religion can bring out the historical importance of obedience to God-given norms of action, to the "natural laws for human society," and to inspiration. The parable of the pounds or talents (Luke 19:12-27; Matthew 25:14-30) brings out the inequality of gifts and endowments, and shows how the ungifted rebel out of jealousy. The biological and marital statutes of the Jewish Law are examples of the historical importance of respect for biological factors.

11. There has never been a primitive community or society

without private property. We have proof of this in the objects found in graves from as early as the Neanderthal period, and in the fact that every child has a possessive instinct which finds expression even before the child can speak properly. Behavioral research shows that the instinct to possess and own is present in all species of animals as part of the drive to sustenance and self-preservation; the instinct is manifested in the form of the "territorial instinct." The elimination of private property will not prevent this drive from expressing itself in the perverted form of greed. The attempt to eradicate any drive that is genetically determined and is necessary for the life of the individual and the community always causes its displacement and perversion and has destructive effects.

The result is always the same, whether it be the Communists attempting by force to get rid of the instinct to acquire property, or Manichean Christians attempting to get rid of the sexual drive, or the Nazis attempting to get rid of the instinct to take flight, or pacifists and pluralists attempting to get rid of the aggressive drive. The attempt to eliminate the urge to acquire property leads to the perversion of that instinct. The production of a people is reduced to a fraction of what it might be; thievery and corruption inevitably follow. Without property there is no freedom from the dictatorship of the State or other power on which we depend. Spiritual and moral freedom is closely bound up with economic freedom. Socialism and Communism therefore lead to universal impoverishment and enslavement.

It is for this reason that Jesus does not take up arms against the instinct to possess property, but rather gives it a higher and abiding goal: "Do not lay up for yourselves treasures on earth, where moth and rust consume and where thieves break in and steal, but lay up for yourselves treasures in heaven" (Matthew 6:19-20). Use the unrighteous mammon, but for the right purposes!

12. Man's basic vital drive is "the will to meaning" (Viktor Frankl) and not the quest for libidinal satisfaction. Men attempt to make sensual satisfaction the goal of the instincts; they look for pleasure instead of trying, in accordance with the created order, to follow the basic orientation of each instinct or drive (the conservation of life in the drive for food and possessions; the preservation of the species in the reproductive instinct; protection and the

great enterprises and goals of the community in the aggressive instinct; the preservation of life in the instinct to flee). The result is the isolation and perversion of pleasure which is meant to be a stimulus to and a "reward" for the attainment of the goals assigned by nature to the drives, and which is therefore, even in man, a constitutive element in the structure of the instincts.

When pleasure becomes an end in itself, it becomes diseased and destructive. The "will to authentic meaning" disappears, and there is a loss of meaning when pleasure is thus isolated, a loss of meaning not only for the instincts or drives but for life itself. Behavior that is contrary to the created order, and the elimination from the instincts of components put there by creation, always mean the elimination of the creator as well. The abuse of created gifts and tasks so as to make them yield an isolated pleasure divides man from the creator, and every such separation is sinful.

The uncontrolled quest of libidinal satisfaction, then, excludes authentic meaning and is a denial of sin. This is a theme that should be developed on a biblical basis in the upper grades. What is the ultimate meaning of human life and therefore of man's natural drives as well? Seek first the kingdom of God and its uprightness; then everything else (including supreme joy and pleasure, and an ordered instinctual life) will automatically be yours! God's plan for the family and marriage and for the use of our instinctual powers and our energies is the answer to egoistic perversion and destruction.

13. There is therefore no "emancipation of sexuality," no "right to the acquisition of pleasure" or "right to a successful sex life." Moreover, since the hormonal sex glands do not develop but are inactive from birth to puberty, there is absolutely no need for sexual activity in children.

14. The ability to conceive, bear, nourish, and raise a child is the most wonderful gift a woman possesses, and a gift that until now has remained the most incomprehensible. Menstruation constantly reminds her of this power she has. To describe it as a "weakness" or to say that she is coerced into bearing children is to give proof of abysmal stupidity. It shows contempt for woman as mother and, in the last analysis, for the persons to whom women give birth.

15. It is likewise stupid to label marriage and the forms of human community as the project of repressive and authoritarian social structures rather than as higher organisms for the development of the personality toward higher existential meaning. A parallel would be the desire to break down and eliminate all the higher forms of organization and levels of meaning in the name of an unlimited freedom for the part to seek "self-fulfillment." Then every elemental part, every atom, every molecule, every cell (acting now, of course, as a cancer cell), etc., would be liberated from all meaning-giving repression and would be able to "fulfill itself" by breaking out of the higher order and level of life (in which alone it can find a higher meaning and the fulfillment of its highest destiny) and destroying the superior organism! As a matter of fact, the real issue is never "self-fulfillment," but always "fulfillment of meaning." In biblical terms: redemption means liberation from every false tie, and a total association with and integration into God's organism, his kingdom, so that one becomes a member of Christ's body, a branch on the vine, and so on.

The natural law already mentioned (no. 3, above) applies to man in his quest for the fulfillment of meaning: The part attains to a higher level of existence and life within a superior whole by allowing itself to be integrated into that whole. To this end, it must surrender its unconnectedness, freedom of movement, and isolated individuality. The tendency to a higher level of existence, the capacity for integration into a superior organism, and the will to higher meaning: these are the basic tendency and radical thrust of every existent thing, since it is created for ultimate meaning, that is, for community with God. This thrust becomes personal in man, who is capable of entering the closest and highest of unions in the form of love. (Romans 8:19, "Creation waits with eager longing [= this innermost drive] for the revealing of the sons of God.") Love of God means allowing oneself, through a free decision, to be totally integrated into the kingdom of God.

It is not only man who is capable of rebelling against the higher form of existence and the superior organism (a rebellion which, when it is a conscious decision, we call "sin"). We know of comparable rebellions throughout the created order, and call them "sickness." There is the rebellion of organs (stomach disease, heart disease, nerve disease, etc.); the rebellion of molecules (viral diseases); the rebellion of atoms and elemental parts in the electronic realm (mental illnesses). Sin is thus conscious rebellion, and illness is rebellion in the realm of being, against the order established by God and against a higher organism. Death is both the wages of sin and the consequence of rebellion whether in consciousness or in being. In religious instruction, the relation of the elements of nature to the laws of nature can be used to bring out this identity between the modern scientific understanding of disease and the biblical view of sin. My question is: Has anyone been doing this?

Every higher form of existence requires structures and an ordering functioning that correspond to its meaning and finalities. If you really want a higher life, you must accept the structures and functions required for attaining it. This principle holds for marriage and family as forms of sexual integration.

16. From this standpoint there are no "oral, anal, and genital phases" in the development of sexuality in children. Thumb sucking, for example, is connected not with the reproductive instinct but with the nutritional instinct and the pleasure that accompanies its satisfaction. The child in the mother's womb is already sucking its thumb at the age of four months, in order to develop the muscles of the mouth for sucking, so that after birth it can draw milk from the mother's breast. Sigmund Freud had no inkling of this fact. In his convulsive effort to connect all sensual satisfaction with the sexual drive, he simplistically transfers necessary functions such as suckling and thumb sucking from the nutritional drive to "oral sexuality"—and this sort of nonsense is now a "dogma"!

17. The reproductive drive and the aggressive instinct are found throughout nature as distinct and independent drives. (cf. behavioral research; K. Lorenz, *Das sogennante Böse*; Munich: Piper, 1972). The inability to bring the sexual drive under the control of the person is usually accompanied by the inability to master the drive for food and possessions, the instinct to flee and to be aggressive. The result is manifold combinations of gluttony

and sexual excess, or drunkenness, avarice, and irascibility, or aggressive hatred and flight from responsibility and risk, to the point even of flight from life itself.

Consequently, it is entirely arbitrary and false to attempt to reduce all drives to the sexual. It is time for our parish priests, teachers of religion, and social workers, as well as family counsellors, to free themselves from these reactionary and false neo-Freudian ideas. Then they will be able to set forth a scientific theory of the drives and to defend hypotheses that are consistent with the Gospel and not contradictory to it. They will cease to undermine the faith with the false teachings of Kentler, Goldstein, Wrage, Keil, Amend, Leist, and others, and will not find themselves presenting a false doctrine of the drives and, with it, using religious instruction to defend incontinence, impurity, homosexuality, pornography, masturbation, premarital sex, and so forth as "enlightened views of sex"! When we isolate and radically separate the basic creative and lifegiving function of sexuality and the reproductive instinct from the pleasure associated with its exercise, we are in reality excluding the creator himself and turning men into sinners who are incapable of "seeing God" and grasping his existence.

18. The connection between purity and knowledge of God must be given a central place in today's religious instruction. A young person will realize the need of sexual discipline when he or she comes to understand that communion with God is the presupposition of all meaningful existential fulfillment and that the ability to "see God," his plan and will, his goodness, love, and justice is decisive when it comes to perceiving and replying to the false ideologies that lead men astray by perverting the meaning of human existence.

All sexual education must have its basis in a grasp of the tri-unity proper to human sexuality. The three interrelated meanings and aspects of human sexuality are these: (1) The creation of new human life and the preservation of the species; (2) an all-embracing unity that has spiritual and psychic, bodily, economic, and even juridical dimensions (the married couple is a juridical person, a higher whole); and (3) the experience of joy, beauty, and ecstasy due to the fulfillment of the whole sensual part of the person. The purpose of sex education, therefore, must always be the integration of instinct into a higher order and fulfillment of meaning, that is, into the person as a whole and into the "superperson" that is the couple.

Instruction in sex techniques, sexual perversions, and contraception, on the other hand, always awakens a sense of sexual need and turns appetite in the direction of isolating pleasure from the fulfillment of the true meaning of sexuality. When the basic creative function of human sexuality is radically and in principle excluded from the relationship of man and wife, the creator himself is being excluded from the relationship. The opposite of this exclusion of God from the all-embracing communion of man and wife is the integration of sexuality into the "plan" and will of God.

The aim of religious instruction, in this area, should be to approach sexuality from the viewpoint of *religio*, that is, the "binding" of it to God and his plan. "Family planning" is thus a question that is not to be asked and answered in accordance with immediate material or psychological considerations, but must begin long before marriage. How can young people learn to find God's plan for them, and decide whether they should marry at all or rather devote all their creative energies to the "kingdom of God"? If they should indeed marry, how are they to find the partner destined for them? If they find the partner, when should they marry: at twenty? at twenty-seven? at some other age? How many children should they have? Should the wife work?

If God has no plan when it comes to these decisive questions of human life, or if we are not in a position to find out what the plan is and act accordingly, then what is the point of any instruction in "religion," that is, in our being "bound" to God? If there is no possibility of integrating the sexual drive, before and in marriage, into the person and superperson in accordance with a higher plan, then what is the point of all the talk about God? There would no longer be any "sin," any rebellion against God's will, any knowledge of sin, any forgiveness, any grace, and so on — in fact, any ultimate meaning to life at all.

In this area a kind of hellish circle develops very quickly: The sexual exploitation of one's own body or another's for purposes of sexual abreaction or pleasure — in short, impurity of motive — leads to the sullying of the "heart." Impurity of heart in turn makes man incapable of "seeing God," just as untruthfulness makes him incapable of "hearing the voice of Christ." But blindness and deafness to the existence of God leads to atheism and nihilism! It is never science that leads to these isms. The loss of any meaning in life, to which that blindness and deafness has led, causes in turn an inability to integrate the instincts into our life and allows them to take diseased forms. Spiritual blindness and deafness to the existence of God thus becomes ever more total.

Who shall break through this hellish circle? Here is where the teacher of religion must play his or her part in sex education. There are numerous opportunities of showing the intrinsic connections between sexual rebellion and perversion, on the one hand, and, on the other, the loss of religious, cultural, economic, political, military, etc., meaning and the decline of individuals and cultures. It is easy to illustrate from the Bible the struggle of the prophets against the destruction of monotheism and against the idols that were sexual symbols, and the cults devoted to them.

The loss of meaning for, and restraint upon, the reproductive energies of the individual cell in the organism, once the pattern in the nucleus of the cell has been destroyed, brings to light a law of self-destruction that is identical in nature and structure with the law governing the destruction of cultures through unrestrained sexuality. An understanding of purity as a basic law governing the life of all higher organisms and structures, and an understanding of its psychological consequences, can play an essential role in strengthening the motivation of young people and developing a determination to bring their drives under control.

The transformation of creative energies into intellectual, religious, cultural, political, economic, and athletic accomplishments is something that must be taught. The will to meaning and a higher level of existence must not be obstructed or warped. To purify and develop it should be a key task of religious education. Family planning? Yes, but according to God's plan, not according to the personal self-centered plans of the partners.

19. Pornography makes human beings incapable of love and marriage. It does so because it is a way of programming the un-

conscious exclusively with patterns of sexual behavior in which the person regards his own body and the body of the other solely as a means of pleasure and thus renders impossible the kind of total love between man and wife that leads to complete spiritual, psychic, and bodily oneness. Since such an all-embracing love cannot be shared with a third party and belongs solely to the two lovers, it cannot be shown in films or photographs. When other eyes feast upon it, it immediately becomes a means of abreaction and stimulation for others, and is perverted into a form of exhibitionism and prostitution. The total act of love cannot be shown in a picture; the "act of love" that is shown has been perverted in its very essence into radical self-centeredness and exploitation.

In consequence, there is a special law governing sexual pictures that does not hold for pictures of criminal activities. As regards the latter, it is also possible to show in pictures the opposite kind of behavior, so that the unconscious need not inevitably be programmed solely with one-sided patterns of behavior. It is impossible, however, to show a total love in a picture; any attempt to picture it essentially perverts it.

It is therefore also impossible to counterbalance the false programming of the unconscious through perverted patterns of sexual behavior, and to preserve a freedom of choice between pictures and behavioral patterns in the unconscious. Sexuality is inevitably educated in the wrong direction; inevitable, too, wherever pornographic pictures are on the market, is an increase in the number of serious sexual crimes and divorces (Dr. Court, University of Adelaide, Australia, 1975).

Pornography is socially harmful and must therefore continue to be prohibited. This has long been realized, and the realization led to international agreements and treaties — not just between Christian nations — which the German Federal Republic has now broken (including agreements with States of the communist bloc). Harm is done to individuals and families, but we must now add the harm done to international relations by the self-effected destruction of the credibility of individuals and cultures. By this I mean that the public onslaught on the dignity of woman and on the mystery veiling the origin of human life makes the nation that indulges in it contemptible and sordid in the eyes of other people.

Yet, in the atomic age, the basis of any true peace can only be a mutual respect for each other as human beings, a mutual respect for the dignity of men! There can thus be no more potent argument against freedom than the self-disfigurement a nation inflicts on itself before the eyes of others. Contempt, hatred, even a desire to destroy are the feelings roused in others who reject pornography. The justification of totalitarianisms is always that freedom has disqualified itself.

No one has the right to spread the germs of smallpox or typhoid fever. We have accurate knowledge today of how corrupt models of behavior affect general attitudes; we know the "infectious" working of erroneous psychic behavior. The layman is incapable of recognizing and judging the effects of invisible bacilli and viruses. The same holds for infectious pictures. It is not enough to be "mature" or to think one can take into one's mind everything that is "natural" without suffering harmful effects. The knowledge that an infected object is harmful is no protection against the infection; the object must be disinfected and disposed of. This last, however, is the duty of the State.

Jesus was well aware of the effects of the sexually aroused look: "Every one who looks at a woman lustfully has already committed adultery with her in his heart" (Matthew 5:28). He is not here proposing a "narrow and repressive outlook." He is simply telling us not to befoul our own inner world, for this destroys our ability to "see God" and realize his existence and respond to his inspiration, just as a cell that has become blocked up is no longer able to react to the higher, meaning-giving impulses from our bodies and spirits.

20. It is radically false to claim that the essential cause of belief in God is the extrapolation of the fear men feel at the uncontrolled forces of nature and especially in the face of death. The decisive cause, on the contrary, is the experience of inspiration (Abraham and Moses used to speak with God as with a friend). Furthermore, all the great religions know that purity and inspiration are linked. Professor I. D. Unwin, of Oxford, a sociologist, ethnologist, and disciple of Freud, has shown the direct connection that exists between premarital continence, sexual discipline (energy for social purposes), and cultural development.

It is also the case that without premarital continence a person never develops an authentic faith in God, and that once sexual discipline has been abandoned, a culture disappears in the third generation and falls back into polytheism, demon worship, and so forth. Had it not been for the bloody centuries-long struggle of the prophets against the sexual cults of Canaan, monotheism would never have survived in Israel. Monotheism is always the result of personal inspiration, of the experience of being addressed by God, and of an I-Thou relationship with him. Fear of death and of the powers of nature cannot beget a monotheistic belief in God. In the contemporary teaching of religion it is essential that these various connections be brought out.

Only when there is readiness to attempt the "experiment with God" and when there has been an experience of the reality of God's guidance and divine plan, can a person also experience in a truly existential way the breaking of this relationship with God. The break occurs through rebellion and disobedience to the known will of God. Sin is therefore not simply a feeling of one's infirmity, but a force that leads to a complete destruction of the relationship. In consequence, sin casts man down from a higher level of existence, isolates him, and launches him out without a rudder on a sea of meaninglessness. But the experience of the re-establishment of the relationship can be just as real; it takes place through acknowledgment and confession of sin, hatred and abandonment of it, and reparation for it, in short, through grace and forgiveness. Since all these are experiences everyone can have who places the "necessary conditions" and is ready to seek fulfillment at the highest level of meaning, they are in no sense mere forms of "self-deception," but embody the working out of a natural law that we have already seen to apply to all the higher levels of existence.

21. Education without coercion or fear endeavors to convince through argument; it appeals solely to the mind and attempts to explain everything. Such an approach is vitiated by a basic error regarding the nature of man, for it ignores the complexity and contradictoriness of our reactions and inherited structures. We can be kept from disregard of God and our fellow men only by a "reverential fear" of God's majesty and of the divine law with respect to our "neighbor." The "fear of the Lord" is still "the be-

ginning of wisdom" and the most effective motive in overcoming our fear of men. When a teacher is "authorized" by God and the student's reverential fear of God, he then possesses a genuine authority and can use a certain amount of coercion without causing harm. Man's urge to flee can be made part of the motivational process and can produce positive results.

Education without coercion or fear is in danger of producing the insolent, arrogant, undisciplined type of person who completely fails to realize the dangers that threaten him, or his own real dependence and limitations. Such a person is estranged from reality and incapable of learning; he resembles an animal in which rabies has destroyed the urge to flee; the animal is unable to scent danger and ends up becoming a victim. The Nazi attempt to kill the urge to flee in the German people led to this kind of arrogance, estrangement from reality, blindness to their own real potentialities and to the dangers that threatened, and eventually brought catastrophe on the entire nation.

Education without coercion or fear is not a Christian objective. A Christian teacher aims to educate men to fear of God and submission to his will and plan. Neither an authoritarian nor an antiauthoritarian, purely human education, but the restoration of God's authority over the whole man and the whole of human society must be the goal of religious instruction.

Summation

In this essay on the question of religious instruction in our day, especially at the upper levels of the school, our aim has been to single out some hypotheses in the natural sciences and psychology that are frequently regarded today as providing a "scientific" basis for the materialist view of the world. We then indicated the need and possibility of responding to them with more correct and scientifically defensible hypotheses. In my experience, too little effort has been made in contemporary religious education to face up to this task and opportunity, or else the task has been approached in an unsatisfactory way.

It is quite possible today to get rid of outdated materialistic and pseudoscientific hypotheses and articles of faith and to replace them with better and scientifically unobjectionable answers. Once these false principles of materialism have been refuted and eliminated, it will be possible to take a much more positive approach and to present the biblical answer.

The introduction of these alternative viewpoints into religious instruction (according to the age of the students and the program they are following) requires a corresponding special formation for teachers of religion and theologians. I know thus far of no institute that deals comprehensively with the response to the pseudo-scientific hypotheses and theories of which I have been speaking and with their misleading ideological conclusions. There is a resultant lack, as far as I know, of relevant literature and books for religious instruction that would handle the subject. The invasion of neo-Freudian theses, Marxist conceptions, and atheistic views in physics, chemistry, biology, psychology, etc., is not being resisted as it should by Christians.

It follows that the models of man, his nature, and his destiny which underlie the ideal proposed for a given society bear largely the impress of pseudoscientific reasoning and ideas. The widespread perplexity is therefore steadily increasing, and it is incumbent on us to respond to the situation on the basis of an alternative, carefully elaborated picture of man and the world that has a solid biblical and scientific foundation.

At this point we must inevitably face up to the difficult conflict that is polarizing the Church in our time. I mean the seeming incompatibility of Christian faith and any ideology. We find two extremes in the Church. One is that section of the community that is concerned solely with assuring their personal salvation and redemption and therefore withdraws from "the world" into private religiosity and piety. The other recognizes the need of changing the very structures of society so that life may become properly human; it therefore plunges into ideological activities and suddenly finds that it is providing the needed "fresh horses" and "useful fools" for antichristian ideologists.

The solution to this unfortunate polarization seems to me to be the following. On the one hand, we must not go along with the idea of simply de-ideologizing the Christian message, for if we do, we sacrifice God's command, "Make disciples of all nations [this includes their economic, political, cultural, etc., structures and principles of action]!" We sacrifice the "Seek first the kingdom of God and its uprightness," and the royal rule of Christ, the Pantocrator of the eastern Church. On the other hand, neither may we accept an ideologization of certain imperfect ideals, such as the idea of a Kingdom of God or a City of God in which various abstractions such as freedom (liberalism), nation (nationalism), social justice (socialism and communism), biological life and race (racial socialism), or peace and brotherly love (pacifism and humanism) are isolated from their proper context, absolutized, and turned into idols.

If we are not to succumb to the second of these two dangers, which is fatal to a Christian civilization, it is vitally important that we learn to combat these partial truths (which are also partial lies) and the incorrect and reactionary pseudoscientific hypotheses on which they rest. We must replace them with superior hypotheses and a comprehensive truth that will provide a rounded picture of human existence as it really is. A proper conception of the "kingdom of God" is one in which all values once again fall into their proper order under the supreme value, which is expressed in "You shall love the Lord your God with all your heart and soul and mind, and your neighbor as yourself." Such a conception allows for the personal dimension required by the knowledge of revelation and the experience of faith, but it also has room for the assertion of God's claim over the nations of the earth and the entire social and political sphere.

The ideological aspect (thus conceived) of the Christian message relates both to the individual and to the world in its entirety. It can, however, credibly claim universal validity only if its ultimate goal, its principles of action, and its structures — in short, the entire model — can be derived not only from revelation and faith but also from contemporary scientific knowledge. If the ideological side of the Christian message concerning God's kingdom can be thus derived, it will indeed be solidly established.

It is clear, of course, that in this process of derivation science must play a secondary role, because even today our scientific knowledge is fragmentary. However, once modern science has been used to correct yesterday's scientific errors and the ideological conclusions drawn from them, there is absolutely no reason why the complete personal and ideological message of God's rule should not be proposed as the sole answer to the antichristian ideologies that are enslaving mankind and destroying the world.

All materialistic ideologies proclaim a revolution against God that is based on class and race, and affects the individual, the family, and the nation. Only where there is an alternative to this revolution can the concepts of "sin," apostasy from God, judgment, redemption, and grace be applied to peoples, classes, and races, as well as to individuals.

Partial truths and partial ideals that are turned into idols and end up destroying man prove to be ideological straitjackets. An alternative is needed: the message of a world order and an "ideology" that are liberating and redemptive, that embrace the whole man, and that are inspired by God. This alternative must be presented in a way that is intelligible to contemporary man. But the alternative to sin and rebellion against God by individual and society can be put forth in a credible way only if Christians provide models and exemplars, if they let their light shine before men, and if both in practice and in theory (or vision) their plan is superior to that offered by deluded preachers and false prophets.

Such a course of action requires the courage to go forward despite the automatic persecution that will come from the seemingly almighty ideologies of the day, and without concern for external success or failure. The evangelical call for decision that is addressed to individuals and peoples and bids them abandon their false gods and ideological half-truths, their individualism, liberalism, nationalism, socialism, and racism (in short, their collective self-centeredness), and submit to God's commandments and rule — this call may reach the ears of men and lead them to conversion and salvation.

On the other hand, men may follow the path that leads to total rebellion against God and self-annihilation. In either event, the persons proclaiming the message must heed the words: "When these things begin to take place, look up and raise your heads, because your redemption is drawing near" (Luke 21:28).

The task of Christian religious instruction is to show our young people, who have been led astray by deluded ideologues, that the goal of history is not Marxism or socialism or any ism at all. They must be brought to see that the only way to avoid catastrophe today and restore to mankind its true role and destiny has been, is now, and will always be to accept the fully personal yet world-embracing ideological message of God's rule as achieved through the transformation of men's attitudes (not just their outward behavior!) and through belief in the good news (Mark 1:15).

BIBLIOGRAPHICAL REFERENCES

[1] Konrad Lorenz, *Das sogenannte Boese*. Piper Verlag. 1972.

[2] Viktor Frankl, *Theorie und Therapie der Neurosen*. Verlag Urban und Schwarzenberg, Munich-Vienna. 1967.

[3] Julian Huxley, *Evolution in Action*. Harper and Row, New York. 1953.

[4] Paul Campbell, *Modernizing Man*. Grosvenor Books. 1968.

[5] *Sexfibel*. C. W. Leske Verlag, Opladen. 1972.

[6] *Sexualkundeatlas*. C. W. Leske Verlag, Opladen. 1972.

[7] Klaus Verch, *Sexualerziehung*. Verlag St. Augustus. 1971.

[8] Wilhelm Weischedel, *Der Gott der Philosophen*. Wissenschaftl. Buchgesellsch., Darmstadt. 1972.

[9] Siegmund Freud, *Gesammelte Werke*. Verlag S. Fischer, Frankfurt/Main. Band XI, 213. 1966.

[10] George F. Gilder, *Sexual Suicide*. Quadrangle/The New York Times Book Co., New York. 1974.

[11] Wilhelm Reich, *Die sexuelle Revolution*. Europ. Verlagsanstalt.

[12] Paul Marx, *The Death Peddlers — War on the Unborn*. The Liturgical Press, Collegeville, Minnesota. 1973.

[13] Helmut Koester, *Aerztliche Ueberlegungen zur Enzyklika Humanae Vitae*. Vortrag auf dem 2. Aerztetag des Bistums Essen 20. 11. 68. Stimmen der Zeit, 1969, 217.

[14] Kinsey, *Das Sexuelle Verhalten des Mannes*. Fischer Verlag.

[15] Viktor Frankl, *Psychosexuelle Stoerungen*. Oesterr. Aerzte-Zeitung 20, Heft 1, 10.1.56.

[16] Georg Siegmund, *Die Natur der menschl. Sexualitaet*. Naumann Verlag, Wuerzburg. 1972.

[17] *Hollaendischer Katechismus*. Decker und van de Vegt, Nijmegen-Utrecht. 1968.

[18] F. Boeckle, *Sexualitaet und sittliche Norm*, Stimmen der Zeit 1967, 249–266.

[19] *Ulmer Aerztedenkschrift*. Deutsches Aerzteblatt 2.10.65.

[20] H. J. Campbell, *Correlative Physiologie des Nervensystems*. Academic Press. 1965.

[21] Viktor Frankl, *Der Wille zum Sinn*. Verlag Huber, Bern. 1970.

[22] Willhart Schlegel, *Der homosexuelle Naechste*. Furcheverlag. 1965.

[23] Rajmohan Gandhi. Himmat. Panschgani, India. 1968.

[24] *Die Welt* (Tageszeitung). 5.9.1970.

[25] Caux Informationsdienst. 1969.

[26] Karl Gunning, *World Population and the Physiology of Humanity*. Geloof en Wetenschap, Holland. June–July, 1971.

[27] Frank N. D. Buchman, *Fuer eine Neue Welt*. Caux Verlag, Lucerne. 1955.

[28] Carl Friedrich von Weizsaecher, *Rede in der Paulskirche*. 1963.

[29] Professor Picht, *Mut zur Utopie*. Piper Verlag. 1968.

[30] Pasqual Jordan, *Wissenschaft und Geschichte*. 1955.

[31] Aleksandr Solzhenitsyn, *Offener Brief*. Luchterhand. 1974.

[32] I. D. Unwin, *Sex and Culture*. Oxford University Press. 1934.

[33] Pitirim Sorokin, *The American Sex Revolution*. Sargent, Boston. 1956.

[34] *EKD-Denkschrift zu Fragen der Sexualethik*. Guetersloher Verlagshaus. 1971.

[35] Theodor Bovet, *Das Geheimnis ist gross*. Katzmannverlag. 1955.

[36] Wolfgang Wickler, *Das Missverstaendnis der Natur des ehelichen Aktes in der Moraltheologie*. Stimmen der Zeit 1968, 268.

[37] Deutsches Aerzteblatt 1969. *Diskussion ueber Enzyklika H. V.*, 2462 Mediz.-biolog. Stellungnahme der Kath. Aerzteschaft.

[38] Dr. J. Roetzer, *Kinderzahl und Liebesehe*. Herder Verlag. 1972.

[39] Dr. med. Eberhard Sievers, *Empfaengnisverhuetung und andere Sexualprobleme*. Johann Wilhelm Naumann Verlag, Wuerzburg. 1972.

[40] Mary Rosera Joyce, *Love Responds to Life*. Prow Publishers, Kenosha, Wisconsin. 1971.

[41] Prof. Dantine, *Plaedoyer fuer das Selbstbestimmungsrecht der Frau*. Lutherische Monatsschrift Nr. 1, 1973.

[42] J. David, Deutsches Aerzteblatt 1968, bzw. "Orientierung," 31.8.1969.

[43] Peter Riga, *Humanae Vitae and the New Sexuality*. Triumph. October 1973.

[44] Ann Woolrich Gordon, *Peter Howard — Life and Letters*. Caux Verlag, Lucerne. 1970.

[45] Hans Kueng, *Unfehlbar, eine Anfrage*. Benziger Verlag. 1973.

[46] Prof. Dr. Hermann Knaus, *Die fruchtbaren und unfruchtbaren Tage der Frau*. Urban und Schwarzenberg Verlag, Munich-Berlin.

[47] S. Ernst, *Gegen die progressive Sexparalyse der Freiheit*. Verlag Aktion Ulm. 1971.

[48] S. Ernst — Dr. Hilt, *Denkschrift gegen gespaltenes Denken*. Aktion Ulm 70. 1972.

[49] Karl Heim, *Glaube und Denken*. Furcheverlag, Tuebingen. 1938.

[50] Werner Heisenberg, *Der Teil und das Ganze*. Piper Verlag. 1971.

[51] Bernhard Philberth, *Der Dreieine*. Christiana Verlag, Stein a. Rhein. 1974.

[52] Bernhard Philberth, *Christliche Prophetie und Nuklearenergie*. Brockhaus Verlag. 1968.

[53] Dr. Basilea Schlink, *Zum ersten Mal, seitdem es Kirche Christi gibt*. Verlag Evang. Marienschwesternschaft, Darmstadt. 1972.

[54] Peter Howard, *The Secret of Frank Buchman*. Caux Verlag.

Alfred Rust, *Handwerkliches Koennen und Lebensweise des Steinzeit-menschen.* Mannheimer Forum 1973/1974.

Dossenbach und Buehrer, *Von Liebe und Ehe der Voegel.* Verlag C. J. Bucher, Lucerne. 1974.

Pasqual Jordan, *Naturwissenschaft vor der religioesen Frage.* Stallin Verlag. 1970.

H. G. Studnitz, *Ist Gott Mitlaeufer?* Seewaldverlag. 1969.

Peter Howard, *Amerika braucht eine Ideologie.* Verlag Deutscher Buchdienst.

Pasqual Jordan, *Naturwissenschaft und christlicher Glaube.* 1970.

Pope Paul VI, *Zusatzerklaerung zur Enzyklika* Humanae Vitae. 1968.

Paul Roemhild, *Weltbild und Glaube.* Evang. Luth. Volkshochschule Alexandersbad. 1970.

Paul Roemhild, *Am Anfang schuf Gott Himmel und Erde.* Schoepfung und Naturwissenschaft. Alexandersbader Hefte, 1972.

Ernst Ell, *Dynamische Sexualmoral.* Benziger Verlag. 1972.

W. Schoellgen, *Moral fragwuerdig.* Roborverlag Hueckeswagen. 1967.

Kurt Port, *Sexdiktatur.* Portverlag, Esslingen/N. 1972.

Dr. and Mrs. Willke, *Handbook on Abortion.* Hiltz Publishing Co., Cincinnati, Ohio. 1973.

Dr. John Billings, *Natural Family Planning.* The Liturgical Press, Collegeville, Minnesota. 1973.

M. R. Joyce and R. E. Joyce, *New Dynamics in Sexual Love.* The Liturgical Press, Collegeville, Minnesota. 1970.

Dr. med. Sievers, *Natur und Enzyklika.* Johann Wilhelm Naumann Verlag, Wuerzburg. 1969.

Dr. med. Sievers, *Wege zur natuerlichen Empfaengnisverhuetung.* Johann Wilhelm Naumann Verlag, Wuerzburg. 1969.

Irmela Hoffman, *Lebensiaenglich.* Aussaat Verlag, Wuppertal. 1972.

Klaus Bockmuehl, *Atheismus in der Christenheit.* Aussaat Verlag. 1969.

Joerg Gutzwiller, *Mensch Gott Welt.* Theolog. Verlag, Zuerich. 1971.

Erwin Straus, *Psychologie der menschlichenWelt.* Gesammelte Schriften. Springer Verlag Goettinger. 1960.

Balthasar Staehelin, *Urvertrauen und zweite Wirklichkeit.* Editio Academica Zuerich. 1973.

Memorandum der Europaeischen Aerzteaktion an die Europaeischen Parlamente zur Abtreibungsfrage. Verlag Aktion Ulm 70. Ulm, Postfach 672. 1973.

Gemeinsame Erklaerung der Moraltheologen der Bundesrepublik Deutschland v. 27.4.1974.

Protokolle Deutscher Bundestag, Pornographiehearing. November 1971.

Demokratie und Freie Liebe, Denkschrift von 140 schwedischen Aerzten an den Koenig. Deutsche Tagespost, Wuerzburg, 8.1.1966.